ASSESSING GCSE ENGLISH

A Practical Approach to

READING SKILLS

Jean Evans

First published in 2003 by:
Nelson Thornes Ltd
Delta Place
27 Bath Road
CHELTENHAM
GL53 7TH
United Kingdom

03 04 05 06 07 / 10 9 8 7 6 5 4 3 2 1

A catalogue record for this book is available from the British Library

ISBN 0 7487 7462 9

Developed and produced by Start to Finish

Typeset by Paul Manning
Printed and bound in Spain by Graficas Estella

Contents

Introduction

GCSE English has four elements: Reading, Writing, Speaking and Listening. This book focuses on the Reading element and comprises two sections:

- Section 1: Media and non-fiction texts
- Section 2: Poetry from different cultures.

There are twelve units in each section, each concerned with aspects of the skills you need for GCSE. As you work through the activities in each unit, you will develop these skills. And as you work through the units, you will build on the skills, so that by the time you reach the final units in the section, you should be able to put all the skills together to write an answer to an exam-style question.

Media and non-fiction texts

The best way to prepare for the exam is to read widely, both tabloid and broadsheet newspapers, so that you become familiar with, and understand, the language and techniques used by the writers.

Newspapers, as their name suggests, should give us a certain amount of 'news', i.e. factual accounts of events. The writers of articles also give us their informed opinions about events, but you need to know that what they write is based on knowledge and experience and not just an unfounded assertion of their own political beliefs or private prejudices. So one of the most important aspects of studying media texts is to be able to tell fact from fiction.

Reading newspapers for yourself will give you plenty of opportunity to find out what is good reporting and what is not.

Poetry from different cultures

The better you know the texts you study, the more effective your answers will be. So get to know the poems well by reading and rereading them. This will help you to understand them better, to see the subtleties of meaning more clearly and to be able to remember brief, appropriate quotations in the exam.

Your previous study of poetry will help you when you begin to look at poems from different cultures. It is useful to compare these poems with other poems you are familiar with, to think about how they are similar and how they are different. The other poems you are studying for GCSE English will also give you something with which you can compare the poems from different cultures. This book will give you guidance, as will your teacher, but remember that your own independent judgement is very important. What *you* think about a poem is what matters most to examiners. If you are interested in poetry, there is no better way to become proficient at understanding and analysing it than by reading as much of it as you can, at home and at school.

The study of both poetry and the media can lead to some fascinating debates, because everyone has a different viewpoint. Listening to other people's viewpoints and expressing your own will help you to understand better and to clarify your own views on many things. Looking at non-fiction texts will give you the opportunity to work out the difference between this kind of text and poetry, which is largely a product of the poet's imaginative powers.

The language of both poetry and the media is also fascinating. Although poetry is very different from journalism, they do have some common features. For instance, both use a great deal of descriptive language and metaphor, but in very different ways. As you learn to analyse text, how it has been put together and the effect this has on the reader, you will begin to look at other kinds of texts in more detail, which will increase your understanding and improve your writing skills. The more you read, the wider your vocabulary becomes and the more likely you are to write accurate and fluent English.

Some types of writing will appeal to you less than others. Examiners are quite happy for you to express your honest opinion, as long as you back it up by evidence from the text or texts you are discussing. Candidates sometimes assume that examiners want them to praise all the material presented. In reality, there may well be texts that are far from perfect examples of their genre. When you are asked to compare texts, you may find not only that they present material differently but that you prefer one to the other. The examiners want to know what your preferences are and how well you can explain them.

Above all, remember that the more you enjoy what you are doing, the more likely you are to achieve good results.

Sources and acknowledgements

Unit 1.1: 'Hewitt goes on US TV' by Richard Wallace and Ruki Sayid from *Daily Mirror* (10 January 2003), reprinted by permission of Trinity Mirror; 'Hewitt admits hawking letters' by Stephen Bates from *The Guardian*, reprinted by permission of Guardian Newspapers Ltd; 'Cocoa butter' from *Encyclopaedia Britannica*; from Cheshire Real Nappy Network leaflet (Cheshire County Council); HSBC leaflet 'Accessible banking'; 'Zara's burger king' headline from *The Sun* (14 April 2003), © News International Syndication, 2003, reprinted by permission of the publisher; 'Children held at Guantanamo Bay' headline from *The Guardian* (24 April 2003), reprinted by permission of Guardian Newspapers Ltd; **Unit 1.2:** front page from *Daily Mirror* (11 January 2003), reprinted by permission of Trinity Mirror; front page from *The Guardian* (11 January 2003), reprinted by permission Guardian Newspapers Ltd; 'Justin fury over DJ's "gay" slur' by Brian Flynn from *The Sun* (25 April 2003), © News International Syndication, London, 2003, reprinted by permission of the publisher; 'Tariq Aziz taken into US custody' by Rupert Cornwell from *The Independent* (25 April 2003), reprinted by permission of the publisher; **Unit 1.3:** 'Agassi survives the French rapier' by Stephen Bierley from *The Guardian* (18 January 2003), reprinted by permission of Guardian Newspapers Ltd; 'Kicked out for being a playboy' by Darren Lewis from *Daily Mirror* (11 January 2003), reprinted by permission of Trinity Mirror; **Unit 1.4:** from 'Bloodbath plotted in a slum' by Mike Sullivan and Justine Penrose from *The Sun* (24 January 2003), © News International Syndication, London, 2003, reprinted by permission of the publisher; from 'Anger over student debt burden' by Will Woodward from *The Guardian* (23 January 2003), reprinted by permission of Guardian Newspapers Ltd; **Unit 1.5:** 'Are we sitting safely?' leaflet from Child In-Car-Care Scheme, reprinted by permission of Cheshire County Council, Road Safety Unit; HSBC leaflet 'Relax *you're* in good hands'; entry on 'Cloning' from *Encarta* (encarta.msn.com); **Unit 1.6:** advertisement for Freeserve in *The Sun* (24 January 2003); advertisement for AA car insurance; 'The Great Lunn Poly Getaway' advertisement in *The Sun* (24 January 2003); 'Holiday offer' advertisement in *The Independent on Sunday* (6 April 2003), reprinted by permission of the publisher; 'Ex Student's Union' cartoon by Steve Bell from *The Guardian* (23 January 2003), © Steve Bell, reprinted by permission of Steve Bell; 'How much for just the scarf?' cartoon by Matt from *The Daily Telegraph* (23 January 2003), © Telegraph Group Limited, 2003, reprinted by permission of the publisher; 'He can't get anything right just now ...' cartoon by Mahood from *The Daily Mail* (24 January 2003), reprinted by permission of Atlantic Syndication; **Unit 1.7:** Comment: 'Fighting a war on two fronts' and 'Invisible men' from *Daily Mail* (24 January 2003), reprinted by permission of Atlantic Syndication; Comment: 'Loud voice of the people' from *The Sun* (24 January 2003), © News International Syndication, 2003, reprinted by permission of the publisher; letter from Brian Cavendish to *The Sun* (25 April 2003); letter from Ian Parsons to *The Guardian* (25 April 2003); **Unit 1.8:** from 'How to do just about anything on the Internet' in *Reader's Digest*, © 2002, reprinted by permission of The Reader's Digest Association Ltd; 'Blair on the block', leading article from *The Guardian* (1 February 2003), reprinted by permission of Guardian Newspapers Ltd; '50 Top Tips' to *Radio Times* readers by Alan Titchmarsh; **Unit 1.9:** from 'Earth, winds and fire' by Charlie English from *The Guardian* Travel section (1 February 2003), reprinted by permission of the publisher; from 'Rage of the gods' by Melanie McGrath from *The Guardian* (12 October 2002), reprinted by permission of the publisher; from Pfizer article in *The Guardian*

(24 April 2003); **Unit 1.10:** 'CAF: An Overview' from www.cafonline. org, reprinted by permission of Charities Aid Foundation; 'Getting the giving habit' by Liza Ramrayka from *The Guardian* (26 June 2002), reprinted by permission of the publisher; **Unit 1.11:** 'Reddy Steady Dough' by Tom Worden from *The Sun* (8 February 2003), © News International Syndication, London, 2003, reprinted by permission of the publisher; 'Charities – know your place' by Nick Cater from *The Guardian* (29 October 2002), reprinted by permission of Guardian Newspapers Ltd; **Unit 1.12:** 'And the whinger is ...' by Thomas Whitaker from *The Sun* (15 February 2003), © News International Syndication, London, 2003, reprinted by permission of the publisher; 'Courtroom drama' by Matt Wells from *The Guardian* (11 February 2003), reprinted by permission of the publisher; **Unit 2.1:** 'Island Man' by Grace Nichols from *The Fat Black Woman's Poems* (Virago, 1984), © Grace Nichols 1984, and 'Abra-Cadabra' by Grace Nichols; 'Bwalla the Hunter' by Kath Walker from *The Dawn is at Hand: Selected Poems* (Marion Boyars, 1992), reprinted by permission of the publisher; **Unit 2.2:** 'Limbo' by Edward Kamau Brathwaite from *The Arrivants: A New World Trilogy* (Oxford University Press, 1973); 'Hungry Ghost' by Debjani Chatterjee; 'The Sea' by Yashodhara Mishra; **Unit 2.3:** 'Vultures' by Chinua Achebe from *Beware Soul Brother* (Heinemann African Writers Series, 1972); 'What Were They Like?' by Denise Levertov from *Selected Poems* (Bloodaxe Books, 1986); **Unit 2.4:** 'One Question From a Bullet' by John Agard; 'Presents from My Aunts in Pakistan' by Moniza Alvi from *Carrying My Wife* (Bloodaxe Books, 2000), reprinted by permission of the author; **Unit 2.5:** 'Not My Business' by Niyi Osundare from *Songs of the Seasons* (Heinemann Educational Books, 1990); 'Love After Love' by Derek Walcott from *Collected Poems 1948–1984* (Faber & Faber, 1986), reprinted by permission of the publisher; **Unit 2.6:** 'Tables' by Valerie Bloom; 'Hurricane Hits England' by Grace Nichols from *Sunrise* (Virago, 1996), © Grace Nichols 1996; **Unit 2.7:** 'Search for My Tongue' by Sujata Bhatt from *Brunizem* (Carcanet Press, 1988), reprinted by permission of the publisher; from 'Unrelated Incidents' by Tom Leonard from *Intimate Voices: Selected Works 1965–1983* (Galloping Dog Press, 1984; Vintage Books, 1985); **Unit 2.8:** 'Half-Caste' by John Agard from *Get Back Pimple* (Penguin Books, 1996); **Unit 2.9:** 'Nothing's Changed' by Tatamkhulu Afrika; 'Blessing' by Imtiaz Dharker from *Postcards from God* (Bloodaxe Books, 1997); **Unit 2.10:** 'This Room' by Imtiaz Dharker from *I Speak for the Devil* (Bloodaxe Books, 2001); **Unit 2.12:** 'Two Scavengers in a Truck, Two Beautiful People in a Mercedes' by Lawrence Ferlinghetti (New Directions Publishing Corporation), © 1979 by Lawrence Ferlinghetti, reprinted by permission of the publisher.

Every effort has been made to trace and contact all copyright holders. The publishers would be pleased to rectify any omissions brought to their notice at the earliest opportunity.

Photographs
Action Images/Jason O'Brien, page 20; **The Guardian**, page 15; **The Guardian/Dan Chung**, page 74; **Mirrorpix**, pages 8, 14, 21; **Mission Pictures**, page 73 (Catherine Zeta Jones); **News International Newspapers**, page 67; **Reuters News Agency**, page 73 (Michael Douglas).

Illustrations
Linda Jeffrey, pages 55, 58, 78, 123, 136, 146; **Carol Jonas**, pages 48, 49, 92, 93, 97, 100, 111, 116; **Ruth Palmer**, pages 26, 62, 86, 103, 126, 141

Unit 1.1
Defining media and non-fiction texts

The unit activity is to compare two media texts and two non-fiction texts
(see page 11).

Making a start

'Media' and 'non-fiction' are terms we hear used a great deal, but what exactly do they mean? This unit will define the terms and outline some of the different examples you may come across in your GCSE studies.

Media

The word 'media' is the plural form of the Latin *medium*, which means the form used for doing something. So, for instance, television is a medium for education, entertainment, etc. However, media is generally used as a collective noun for press, television, radio, and so on, and can nowadays be used as either a singular or a plural word.

Finding your way around newspapers

Within the media, there are different kinds of writing that you need to be familiar with and learn to analyse. Newspapers are the most important form of the media that you will encounter. Important aspects of newspapers that you need to study are:

- tabloid newspapers, for example, *Daily Express*, *Daily Mirror*, *Daily Mail*, *The Sun*
- broadsheet newspapers, for example, *The Times*, *The Guardian*, *The Independent*, *The Daily Telegraph*
- different types of articles within tabloid and broadsheet newspapers
- advertisements in both types of newspaper.

Activity 1.1a   Apart from the work you do in and for school, the best way to prepare for work on media texts is to read as many examples as you can find for yourself. If you have a daily or weekly newspaper at home, read that. Try to look at both tabloids and broadsheets even if you only see one kind of paper at home.

Non-fiction texts

'Non-fiction' is quite a difficult word to define. *The Concise Oxford Dictionary* defines it as 'prose writing that is informative or factual rather than fictional'.

The problem is that it is difficult sometimes to work out the difference between what is fictional, i.e. made up or imagined by the author, and what is non-fictional or factual. Non-fiction is based in **fact**, but it also often expresses the **opinion** or viewpoint of the person who is writing it. One of the most important things you have to do is, as the Assessment Objective says, is to 'distinguish between fact and opinion'.

TYPES OF MEDIA

The media you will be most familiar with are:

- newspapers
- magazines
- radio
- television
- the Internet.

The media you have to respond to for your GCSE course are the *written media*, such as newspapers, magazines and the Internet.

TYPES OF NON-FICTION TEXTS

Non-fiction texts include:

- encyclopaedias
- reference books
- articles about such things as geography, nutrition, etc.
- leaflets
- school textbooks.

The most obvious types of non-fiction you are likely to come across in examinations are reference texts, magazine articles and leaflets.

The writer's purpose

The form of a non-fiction text varies depending on the type of text it is, just as the form of a tabloid article is different from the form of an article in a broadsheet newspaper. We shall be looking at a variety of examples of both media texts and non-fiction texts to find out the differences and how to recognise and analyse them.

An encyclopaedia entry, for instance, will usually be in small type and close-packed print with few illustrations unless it is specifically designed for children. A leaflet, on the other hand, will use a variety of fonts, larger type, illustrations and a layout that is interesting and eye-catching.

What this suggests to us as readers is that the way a piece of text is written and laid out is dependent on the reason why the author wrote it – the writer's **purpose**. This might be to inform, entertain, persuade or instruct.

COMPARING BROADSHEET AND TABLOID NEWSPAPERS

The most obvious difference is that a broadsheet has pages twice the size of a tabloid. That is, however, only the beginning of the differences.

Checklist of things to look for

- Size of headlines
- Size of subheadings
- Use of colour
- Use of pictures
- The amount of text compared to the number of pictures
- The number of paragraphs

COMPARING NON-FICTION TEXTS

As with newspapers, you will find that non-fiction texts are very different.

Checklist of things to look for

- The amount of text
- The number of pictures or symbols
- How text and pictures are laid out on the page
- Size of fonts
- Use of headings
- Use of colour

Tabloid

Zara's burger king

Large picture

Brief text

More picture than text

Leaflet

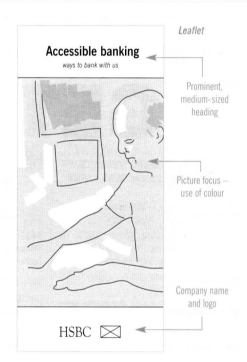

Accessible banking
ways to bank with us

Prominent, medium-sized heading

Picture focus – use of colour

Company name and logo

HSBC

Small heading

Dense print, small font

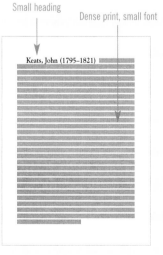

Keats, John (1795–1821)

Biographical dictionary

Medium-sized headline

Focus on text

Broadsheet

Small picture

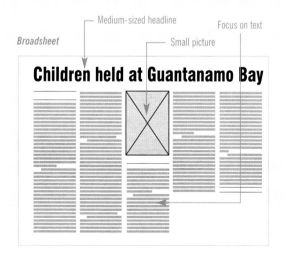

Children held at Guantanamo Bay

Extract
A

Hewitt goes on U.S. TV and vows to sell Di's letters and move to Eastern Europe ...

CONFESSION: Smirking Hewitt tells CNN's Larry King of his plans to quit UK

KIND OFFER: We'll send him by Tupolev jet to remote hut in deepest Siberia

.. but we didn't think that was nearly far enough, so we're buying him a Siberian shack and a one-way ticket to Irkutsk

GET LOST

By RICHARD WALLACE, US Editor, and RUKI SAYID

ROYAL love-rat James Hewitt yesterday said he wanted a fresh start in Eastern Europe, so the Mirror has booked him on a one-way flight...to SIBERIA.

We bought the loathsome cad his ticket on the London-to-Moscow flight after his smarmy performance on US TV, telling chat show host Larry King he WILL sell Diana's love letters.

After his four-hour flight on the Aeroflot Boeing 737, he is scheduled to take an internal flight on a Tupolev TU 154 to Irkutsk, in eastern Siberia.

And though the ticket cost £261, we're also happy to put a deposit on a shack – costing £1,405 – so he has somewhere to rest his weary head.

Hewitt can be sure that,

FOR SALE: Diana's letters

AFFAIR: Lovers Hewitt and Diana

even with temperatures plunging to – 50C, the local welcome will be warmer than the one he gets back in the UK.

During his live interview, the bounder told of plans to leave Britain and cash in on Diana's letters. He said: "I've nothing to be ashamed of. Yes, I would be available to sell them. I'm not being hypocritical – I'm being honest.

"Ideally, it would be to a private collector or a museum. They should be displayed and it would be irresponsible to destroy them."

Hewitt, 44, added: "I don't think that I've

betrayed her. I was utterly faithful to her when she was alive. I've been utterly faithful to her since her death.

"If they went for £10 million, ask yourself who wouldn't think of selling?" The ex-army tank commander has been offered millions for some of the 64 handwritten letters – which he said are in "a safe place abroad" – sent between 1989 and 1991 during their affair.

He said: "I had no intention of selling, but I was approached by someone who offered £5 million for 10 letters.

"I mean, it's a lot of money. And, sadly, the let-

ters have become famous."

But even he acknowledged this would make it hard for him to stay at home.

He said: "I will probably leave England this year to try and make another life somewhere around the Mediterranean or Eastern Europe."

Wearing a navy suit and pale blue shirt, Hewitt went into painstaking detail about his relationship with Diana.

He said: "She was a lonely, unloved woman who needed friendship and love at that time in her life.

"She was beautiful, charming and kind – with a great sense of humour."

Asked if he ever thought of marrying Diana, he said: "It's difficult to say ... there was always a possibility."

He said the media ended the five-year affair, adding: "They found out."

Hewitt again denied rumours he is the real father of Prince Harry. "I think the poor chap has gone through enough. I've said many times I'm not," he said.

And he slammed Paul Burrell and Sarah Ferguson, both of whom have denounced Hewitt on King's show.

Yesterday, the British Library asked to be given the love letters.

Head of manuscripts Dr Christopher Wright said: "It is better such letters are in a major collection where preservation and access is guaranteed."

from Daily Mirror, 10 January 2003

National news

Hewitt admits hawking letters

Stephen Bates

James Hewitt, Princess Diana's lover, admitted yesterday that he wants to sell 64 letters that she wrote to him during their affair in the early 1990s.

The major, who was exposed last month trying to sell the documents for an alleged £10m by the *News of the World*, used a high-profile marketing opportunity on CNN television in the US to claim he was being honest rather than hypocritical. He is understood to be facing bankruptcy proceedings later this month.

He told the cable station's interviewer Larry King: "I think it is important to understand that they are or will become important historical documents. It think it might be irresponsible not to sell them and to generate something one can do some good with. They are extremely well-written, nothing to be ashamed of."

Mr Hewitt, 44, long excoriated in tabloid newspapers as a royal love rat and cad, said he wanted to leave Britain and live abroad. He has already generated considerable income from the affair, receiving £300,000 for cooperating in a book called Princess in Love in 1994 and writing an autobiography, Love and War, detailing the relationship in 1999.

The latest ploy contradicts his insistence nearly five years ago that he would never dream of selling the letters. At that time they were reluctantly returned to him by the royal family, under threat of legal action, after they were handed over by a national newspaper which received them from another of Mr Hewitt's former lovers.

In December he attempted to sell them to an undercover reporter from the News of the World at Claridge's, claiming he had already rejected an offer from an American collector for £5m for 10 of the most salacious letters. The newspaper quoted selectively some of the milder passages before adding: "There are also many sections that we heard read out that we would not dream of publishing."

The letters were written on British forces notepaper by the princess, allegedly signing her name as Julia, to the major while he was serving in the Gulf war. The couple met in 1986, some years after the birth of the princess's two sons, and their affair ended in 1992 at about the time Diana's matrimonial unhappiness was publicly exposed.

There appears to be a ready, and lucrative, market for the princess's memorabilia in the US. Websites sell royal letters and photographs and the recent trial of the former royal butler Paul Burrell was told tales of a mysterious New York millionaire apparently ready to pay large sums for items of her clothing.

No sooner had the major appeared than another figure from the royals' past popped up on CNN. Sarah Ferguson, the former wife of Prince Andrew, claimed that Mr Hewitt had phoned her in New York this week to see if she would like to go out for a drink.

She told Larry King that she had replied: "The answer is no, James, I don't want to have a drink with you. If I did, it would probably end up in the newspaper the next day."

She added: "I think he should just go away. Betrayal, I think, is the most horrible, disloyal thing you can do to anyone."

St James's Palace yesterday declined to comment.

But last night the British Library expressed interest in acquiring the letters, though not in paying the sort of sum Mr Hewitt has been demanding. In a statement the library said it would be an "ideal repository" for the correspondence and said it could respect issues of privacy and the donor's wishes.

from The Guardian, *10 January 2003*

Extract C

cocoa butter, also called THEO-BROMA OIL, pale-yellow, edible vegetable fat obtained from cocoa beans, having a mild chocolate flavour and aroma, and used in the manufacture of chocolate confections, pharmaceutical ointments, and toiletries. It is valued for its melting characteristics, remaining brittle at room temperature or lower but melting just below body temperature. One of the most stable fats known, cocoa butter contains antioxidants that discourage rancidity and allow storage life of two to five years. Its use with other fats improves their stability. Treatment of cocoa butter to remove aroma and colour also removes antioxidants, increasing susceptibility to rancidity.

Cocoa butter is an important component of eating chocolate. Although the chocolate liquor used in manufacturing eating chocolate already contains cocoa butter, an additional amount is required to produce a molded product that remains firm until dissolved in the mouth. The amount of fat obtained from hydraulic pressing of chocolate liquor in cocoa manufacture has become insufficient for the demands of chocolate production, and whole cocoa beans or nibs may be processed mainly for their cocoa butter content. Because of the high cost of cocoa butter, substitutes have been developed, including a type suitable for warm weather because of its higher melting point; such fats, which many countries prohibit in products sold as pure chocolate, impart waxy texture and taste similar to that of cocoa butter. *See also* chocolate.

from Encyclopaedia Britannica

Extract D

Local Authorities are Backing Babies' Bottoms!

Throwaway nappies are not just expensive for parents! The UK alone produces about 800,000 tonnes of nappy waste per year, which local authorities must collect and dispose of. For every £1 spent on "disposables", it costs the taxpayer 10p to dispose of them! The total national cost of this single use, limited customer product is £40 million a year. It is

no surprise that councils are joining the campaign for real nappies.

The chemicals that make up disposable nappies' 'superabsorbent layer' (the gel) are not subject to government controls or independent testing. Superabsorbers were removed from tampons in 1985 because of their link to toxic shock syndrome. The possible effects of extreme dryness on babies' thin skin and reproductive organs remains unstudied. Meanwhile, there is anecdotal evidence about health concerns and these chemicals.

| Protect your baby's skin from unknown chemicals | Easy, hygienic disposal of liner down the loo | Save the UK £40 million in disposal a year |

Extract
D
contd

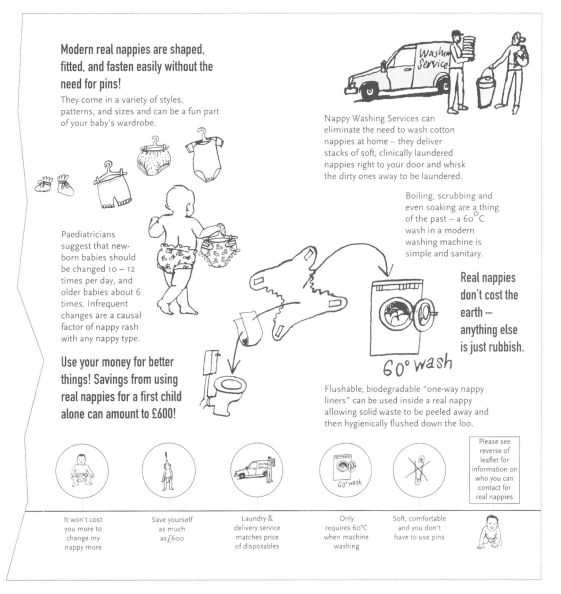

Modern real nappies are shaped, fitted, and fasten easily without the need for pins!

They come in a variety of styles, patterns, and sizes and can be a fun part of your baby's wardrobe.

Paediatricians suggest that new-born babies should be changed 10 – 12 times per day, and older babies about 6 times. Infrequent changes are a causal factor of nappy rash with any nappy type.

Use your money for better things! Savings from using real nappies for a first child alone can amount to £600!

Nappy Washing Services can eliminate the need to wash cotton nappies at home – they deliver stacks of soft, clinically laundered nappies right to your door and whisk the dirty ones away to be laundered.

Boiling, scrubbing and even soaking are a thing of the past – a 60°C wash in a modern washing machine is simple and sanitary.

Real nappies don't cost the earth – anything else is just rubbish.

60° wash

Flushable, biodegradable "one-way nappy liners" can be used inside a real nappy allowing solid waste to be peeled away and then hygienically flushed down the loo.

Please see reverse of leaflet for information on who you can contact for real nappies

| It won't cost you more to change my nappy more | Save yourself as much as £600 | Laundry & delivery service matches price of disposables | Only requires 60°C when machine washing | Soft, comfortable and you don't have to use pins |

from a leaflet published by Cheshire Real Nappy Network

Serious practice

UNIT ACTIVITY 1.1 Work in groups.

1 Look at Extracts A and B. How do you know at a glance that one is from a tabloid and one from a broadsheet newspaper? What are the obvious features that are different, even without examining the wording of the articles themselves?

2 Look for the obvious differences between Extracts C and D which are non-fiction.

WHAT EXAMINERS ARE LOOKING FOR
The examiners want to know that you can see the differences in appearance between pieces of text. The mark scheme would tell examiners to look for 'a clear explanation' of the different layouts of tabloid and broadsheet newspapers for a C grade.

Unit 1.2

Reading newspapers

The unit activity is to analyse and compare the content of tabloid and broadsheet newspapers (see page 17).

Making a start

In Unit 1.1 we considered some of the obvious, visual differences between tabloid and broadsheet newspapers. In this unit, we shall look at those differences in more detail.

Comparing front pages

The front pages of the *Daily Mirror* and *The Guardian* for 11 January 2003 are reproduced on pages 14 and 15. You can see that they are strikingly different.

FEATURES OF NEWSPAPER FRONT PAGES

- The masthead
- The headlines
- The subheadings
- Index or references to other pages in the paper
- The variety of fonts used
- The pictures
- The relationship between pictures and articles
- The number of articles
- Advertising
- Price

USEFUL WORDS

masthead
The area across the top of the front page which gives the paper's name.

font
The particular kind of typeface used, which may vary in size or appearance.

Hint

You should be able to find all of the features on the front page of one of the papers, but fewer in the other.

Activity 1.2a

Look at Extracts A and B. Identify as many of the features of front pages as you can in each one. Copy and complete the table to help you make notes.

Feature	A *Daily Mirror*	B *The Guardian*
Masthead		
Headlines		
Subheadings		
Index or reference to other pages in the paper		
Variety of fonts used		
Pictures		
Relationship between pictures and articles		
Number of articles		
Advertising		
Price		

Mastheads

Every newspaper has a masthead that is used on every issue to make it easily recognisable to its regular readers. In Extracts A and B, the mastheads are in similar-sized fonts – the *Mirror* uses white on black and puts the word 'Mirror' in a larger font size; the *Guardian* uses black on white and puts the word 'Guardian' in a larger font size, while 'The' is in italics.

Headlines and subheadings

The *Mirror's* main headline is 'Throw the key (and him) away' in bold, black capitalised type. The meaning of the headline only emerges through the subheading, which is in smaller type – 'Girl's car killer faces years in jail' – and through the inclusion of the photos of the dead child and her killer.

The Guardian's main headline is 'In the end there was no glory, just a grim death'. The font size is much smaller than that of the main headline in the tabloid, but like the *Mirror's* headline, it relies on a picture and a subheading to make sense to anyone who has not been following the story.

Index or references to other pages in the paper

The Guardian has a number of ways of drawing attention to what is in the rest of the paper:

- a 'Quick Index'
- a reference to 'Monday's G2'
- references to the pages on which front page stories are continued.

The *Mirror* has another major headline – 'O'Leary: I'd make Lee Bowyer captain' – which appears beneath the three words in capitalised blue font 'Shock soccer exclusive'. This refers to an article inside the paper.

The variety of fonts used

Both papers use a variety of fonts. The notable differences between the two papers are that:

- the tabloid makes considerable use of large capitals which are not used by the broadsheet at all
- larger fonts generally are used on the tabloid front page
- the broadsheet makes much more use of small print to give detailed news coverage.

The pictures

It is interesting to see which pictures are chosen. Both papers deal with stories about criminals. *The Guardian* reports the end of a high-profile case of a gunman who held a hostage in a Hackney bedsit for eight days and gives a considerable amount of space to a picture of the gunman. The *Mirror's* story is about a hit-and-run driver, but there is only a small picture of him. The main picture is of former Leeds United manager David O'Leary and Lee Bowyer, former Leeds United player now signed up for West Ham.

Extract **A**

DAILY Mirror

Saturday
January 11 2003

NEWSPAPER OF THE YEAR   45p

GET YOUR **SUNDAY Mirror** FOR JUST 30P
COUPON: PAGE 22

SHOCK SOCCER EXCLUSIVE

O'Leary: I'd make Lee Bowyer captain

SUPPORT: Former Leeds boss David O'Leary is backing Lee Bowyer

BACK PAGE

THROW THE KEY (AND HIM) AWAY

Girl's car killer faces years in jail

By JEREMY ARMSTRONG

THE hit and run car thief who killed six-year-old Rebecca Sawyer could get 17 years' jail.

Ian Carr, 27, pictured left, pleaded guilty yesterday to causing her death by dangerous driving.

He smashed into her dad Steven's car on New Year's Eve. Then he ran off, ignoring injured Steven's cries for help – and leaving Rebecca, right, dead and her 18-month-old sister Kirsty badly hurt. Carr already had a lifetime's driving ban after 89 motoring offences.

And his reckless driving killed his friend Mark Wren in a stolen car in 1990.

Alan Goldsworthy, 29, also in the car when Mark died, said last night: "He will never change. They need to put him behind bars so he can't do this again."

FULL STORY: PAGES 4 & 5

from Daily Mirror, 11 January 2003

Extract **B**

Julian Barnes on Kipling. Review. **Emily Watson** on success. Weekend. **Plus** The Guide

£1
Saturday
January 11 2003
Published in Manchester
and London
guardian.co.uk
* * * *

The Guardian
NORTH

'He was the one politician over the past 50 years whom I have loved'

Roy Jenkins: his final article – in praise of Hugh Gaitskell. Page 20

Cheap Flights to Europe special offer

Travel page 14

In the end there was no glory, just a grim death

Gunman perishes in blaze after 15-day siege costing £1m

Nick Hopkins and
Tania Branigan

Several spells in high security prisons hadn't deterred Eli Hall from living a life of crime. But he had learnt one lesson when he was inside, and this conviction sustained him throughout one of Britain's longest and costliest sieges. Eli Hall wasn't going back to jail.

For 15 days, trained negotiators from Scotland Yard, his aunt, and his hostage, Paul, had tried to persuade him that the demand was unreasonable, but the 32-year-old wouldn't budge. Without the promise he wanted, he bragged that the police "wouldn't take him alive".

And if they tried, he'd go out like Butch and Sundance, both handguns blazing, in the hope of hitting an officer or three.

Hall's stubbornness certainly surprised police. They had hoped that, dispirited by eight days without electricity, six without food and a fortnight without cannabis (the police were advised he had a considerable habit) he would eventually emerge from his bedsit in Marvin Street, Hackney, east London.

But he didn't. He weightlifted to keep warm. His behaviour confounded the 30 to 50 armed officers who had to be on shift duty throughout, the 43 residents trapped in their homes, and the accountants at the Met, who estimate the operation has cost the service up to £1m.

"Every time we thought we were making progress, Eli would get agitated and start taking pot shots," said a source. "Negotiating through the loudhailer became dangerous. It gave him something to aim at."

Looking at Hall's background, police could see he was building up to something, though they didn't regard him as a grade one criminal or a powerful Yardie gangster.

Between 1989 and 1996, Hall, who was born in Jamaica, was arrested on more than 20 occasions for a variety of offences under a variety of different names. He had convictions for violence, drug dealing and carrying offensive weapons and firearms. He'd spent time in Belmarsh prison and had insisted, following his last offence in 1996, for which

he served time in jail, that he would never go back.

Despite the vow, he kept getting into trouble. On May 7 1998, he appeared at Camberwell magistrates court, charged with having sex with an underage girl, though it is unclear how the case ended.

His conduct last year suggested it would only be a matter of time before he emulated either his father, Ranford, who is serving three years for drug offences, or his 17-year-old brother Amias, who was shot dead last summer in Mitcham, south London, in what may

have been a gang feud. Ranford, it seems, was arrested for smoking a joint outside Belmarsh before a visit to see an inmate. The boot of his car was packed with cannabis. Eli's half-brother, Dean, is also in jail.

Detectives had been on Hall's trail long before he barricaded himself in on Boxing Day. He was the chief suspect for the attempted shooting of a police officer in Old Compton Street, Soho, last August.

A similar incident happened in Hackney in July 2001, taking place in a Toyota Celica which was owned by Hall.

By chance, a couple of beat bobbies came across the car during a routine patrol around Hackney over Christmas. Seeing the tow truck arrive to take it away, Hall began to threaten the officers. When an armed team from Scotland Yard's SO19 unit arrived and tried to get into his bedsit, Hall opened fire.

If he had not remonstrated with the police, he would probably still be alive and on the run. Instead, he opted for a confrontation, a decision that told psychiatrists who advised

the police that he was irrational, and potentially dangerously unstable.

Police couldn't rely on the character reference of his neighbours. Some of them had wondered whether the hefty, 30-stone Hall was ill. "You could tell he had mental problems from the way he spoke," said one, who asked not to be named. "He was emotionally wasted." Others expressed amazement that Hall, whom they described as "funny, charming and friendly", was a known criminal.

Ibrahim Tatlises, who runs

the Empire supermarket just around the corner from Marvin Road, occasionally left Hall to mind his shop. "He went jogging at night and in the morning and all he used to eat was peanuts and eggs and drink water. I asked why and he said he was body-building," said one.

Unsure what kind of man they were dealing with, the officers in charge of the police operation, including commanders Mike Messenger, Joe Kaye and Bob Quick, decided not to ▶ **Page 2**

Leader comment, page 23

Eli Hall: he was known to police but not seen as a major criminal. Some neighbours described him as 'charming'

Firearms amnesty to be called

Alan Travis
Home affairs editor

The first national firearms amnesty since the Dunblane massacre will be declared this spring, it was agreed at yesterday's "gun summit" called to tackle Britain's burgeoning gun culture.

Ministers hope that the prospect of a five-year minimum mandatory sentence for carrying an illegal gun will mean that an amnesty will prove more successful than the haul of 15,300 guns which were handed in after the Dunblane massacre or the 48,000 surrendered after the Hungerford tragedy in 1988.

The home secretary, David Blunkett, who chaired the summit held the day after the disclosure that gun crime has surged by 35% in the past 12 months, said an amnesty alone was not a solution. "This is because at the request of the police. Alongside the tougher gun controls announced this week the amnesty will help get many guns off our streets," said Mr Blunkett.

The amnesty was amongst a broad range of new measures agreed at the summit which brought together ministers, police, prosecutors and community leaders. They include:
● giving greater protection to witnesses who testify in gun crime cases, such as separate facilities in court and more video identification parades to tackle the intimidation that prevents them coming forward in the first place;
● encouraging positive anti-gun voices in communities, including among artists in the music industry. This approach has already been used in Jamaica, where Peter Phillips, a former Rastafarian and the minister for national secu-

rity, urged Jamaican artists not to glamorise or glorify violence this week when he launched the annual Rebel Salute stage show;
● the Home Office's police standards unit is to spread successful anti-gun projects including the wider adoption of a "ceasefire strategy" developed in Boston, United States, which has been tried in south Manchester to tackle gang-related gun crime;
● local meetings around the country to develop ways of giving young people an alternative to drug and gun culture.

A follow-up conference will be held in March to see if further legislation is needed to deal with the problem.

Chris Fox, the vice-president of the Association of Chief Police Officers, said the meeting had been entirely positive. "We have a duty to the communities who live in the shadow of gun crime to step up our efforts to root out those who organise and carry out such acts of violence. The solutions, however, lie beyond the power of law enforcement agencies alone," he said.

"It is also about working on youth opportunities and getting jobs and changing the whole view of weapons as a fashion accessory. We will hopefully see some results in the coming months."

But the Tory party leader, Iain Duncan Smith, dismissed the summit as a gimmick: "This did not suddenly rise this year. It has been rising year on year for four or five years. What worries me is that the government has been utterly complacent about this until finally this [week's] set of figures when they have another summit."

Background, page 8

Free with tomorrow's Observer

Observer Sport Monthly

Lee Bowyer Uncovered
Once he was courted by the biggest clubs in European soccer, now he's Britain's football outcast. What makes Bowyer tick? In a searching profile, we reveal the hidden truth about one of the most controversial figures in sport

The Fischer King: Once he ruled the chess world with a

scorching brilliance, now he's plunged into paranoia, bitterness, and hatred of his native America. Rene Chun finally solves the riddle of Bobby Fischer's journey into madness

PLUS: Elena Baltacha ... you might not know the name, but you'll remember the spectacles – of Britain's great tennis hope; the 10 worst decisions in the history of sport; and Hugh McIlvanney on Muhammad Ali

Quick Index
Weather **23**
Quick Crossword **23**
Cryptic Crossword **23**
The Editor, **16**
Today's TV The Guide

02
9 770261 307460
CE ABFPRST

★ Christmas appeal

Last week we asked if you could help us break through the £400,000 barrier for the two charities in our Christmas appeal. You have gone way beyond that and are now heading for the half million mark.

By last night, readers of the Guardian, the Observer, Guardian Weekly and our website, Guardian,Unlimited, had donated £489,328, a generous £54.80 per donor.

Taken together with £3,046 raised from the Guardian choir's carol concert and our

staff "sleaze" raffle of freebies sent to the office by companies and PR firms, that brings us up to £492,474.

Fairbridge, the charity which works with young people in our inner cities, gets £164,322 of that and £328,152 is earmarked for WaterAid, the UK charity dedicated to taking clean water and sanitation to the world's poorest people.

Ravi Narayanan, WaterAid's director, said: "The enormous generosity of readers has far exceeded all our expectations. This support will totally transform people's lives in the developing world. Tens of thousands of people will now gain access to life's most basic needs – clean water and sanitation. Thank you."

Fairbridge's director, Nigel Haynes, was equally warmed by your generosity.

"All of us in Fairbridge," he said, "have been deeply touched by the unexpected and wonderful response to the

Christmas appeal. Sincere thanks."

You can help us match last year's £567,000 by donating this week. The coupon on page 5 gives our postal address, our email address and our telephone number for donations.

Guardian and Observer journalists have revealed the remarkable work of those two charities. We have shown how WaterAid is combating death and disease among the world's poorest people caused by the lack of a basic water supply. At home, we have reported from deprived inner cities, where Fairbridge is helping vulnerable young people overcome the disadvantages of poverty, drug abuse, mental illness and family breakdown.

All of those reports can be read online at guardian.co.uk/christmasappeal.
Please give generously.
Alan Rusbridger, editor

In Monday's G2

Trading places
"My fourth-floor flat shared a dark cul-de-sac landing with two other closed front doors, but all was silent. The doorway had been clamped over with a temporary heavy metal security door.

"It's the crack dealers who move in, set up in a flat and intimidate everyone else," said Jenny."
Polly Toynbee on why she traded her comfortable Victorian house in Clapham for a tiny flat in one of the worst estates in south London

Relationship between pictures and articles

You will notice that a much larger proportion of the tabloid front page is taken up with pictures than with words, whereas the broadsheet is very much the opposite. The main picture on the tabloid front page refers to an exclusive interview inside the paper with David O'Leary. The broadsheet, however, gives detailed coverage of the ending of the Hackney siege, the story and headline framing the gunman's picture.

The number of articles

The Guardian has three articles on the front page, the shortest of which has more than 300 words in it. The *Mirror* has one article of just over 100 words.

Advertising

The only advertising on the front page of the tabloid is for the *Sunday Mirror*. *The Guardian* also advertises its related Sunday paper, *The Observer*, giving details of some of the next day's articles. It also includes an advertisement for a novel just published in paperback.

All we have done so far is observe the differences between the two types of newspapers. You will no doubt also be making deductions about the effects of these techniques on different readers and the purposes of the newspapers' editors and proprietors. We shall go on to consider these in later units.

Activity 1.2b   Find two newspapers published on the same day: a tabloid and a broadsheet. Make your own comparison of the front pages, as above.

The layout of whole newspapers

The front page of the newspaper draws the reader in, but the layout of the rest of the paper is equally important if it is to keep the reader's attention for long enough to persuade him or her buy the paper and to be prepared to buy it again.

COMPARING WHOLE NEWSPAPERS

When comparing whole newspapers, look at the percentage of the paper that is devoted to:

- home news
- international news
- celebrity coverage
- emotive personal stories
- advertising
- cartoons
- sports coverage
- opinion and letters
- obituaries
- reviews.

HARD AND SOFT NEWS

hard news

A term used to describe the coverage of events of national or international importance, such as the situation of the Euro or the actions of Palestinians and Israeli soldiers in their ongoing conflict. See Extract C.

soft news

The kind of news that appeals emotionally to the readers but has little impact on the lives of people generally. Such a story might be about a sick child going to Disneyland or an animal being rescued by the fire brigade. See Extract D.

Extract C

Tariq Aziz taken into US custody

By RUPERT CORNWELL in Washington

Iraq's former foreign minister and deputy prime minister, Tariq Aziz, has been taken into custody, US Central Command in Qatar confirmed last night. He is the highest-profile member of the ousted regime of Saddam Hussein to have fallen into Washington's hands.

Details of his capture were sketchy. According to some reports, Mr Aziz – the best-known face to the outside world of the former regime after Saddam himself – turned himself in. If so, it was not clear where. Nor was it not immediately known where he was being held.

A Chaldean Catholic from the northern city of Mosul, Mr Aziz was neither a Muslim nor a member of the tight clan around Saddam. He made his career within the Baath party and quickly emerged – not least thanks to his excellent English – as the public face of Baghdad's diplomacy, especially in the weeks before the 1991 Gulf War.

Even his foes had a grudging admiration for his presentation skills and his unswerving loyalty to the regime he served.

from The Independent, *25 April 2003*

Extract D

Justin fury over DJ's 'gay' slur

From BRIAN FLYNN in New York

Pop hunk Justin Timberlake slammed down the phone on a live radio show after the DJ asked if he ever had a gay fling.

US shock jock Java Joel started by asking the former NSYNC frontman who was better in bed – his old flame Britney Spears or her rival Christina Aguilera.

The cheeky DJ than demanded to know if Justin, 22, had romped with Kylie Minogue after groping her bum on stage at the Brits.

Fling

But the star went berserk when the Kiss 103.5 presenter asked if he had ever had a homosexual fling with any other members of NSYNC.

The star – dubbed Justin Trousersnake after bragging he was an animal in bed and confessed to losing his virginity at 15 – blasted: "I think you well know the answer to that question."

He fumed: "Any fan of mine does not want to know a dumbass question like 'What are your homo activities?' I can't believe I've wasted my time with you."

He hung up as laughter and applause broke out in the radio studio.

from The Sun, *25 April 2003*

Serious practice

UNIT ACTIVITY 1.2 Find a tabloid newspaper and a broadsheet newspaper for the same day.

1   How many pages does each paper have?
2   Work out roughly how much of each page is devoted to each of the aspects listed above.
3   Work out roughly the percentage of the newspaper devoted to each aspect.
4   Work out how much of each newspaper is devoted to soft news and how much to hard news (see the information above).
5   Compare your results (or those of your group) with others in the class.

Hint

When comparing the number of pages in each paper, remember that a page in a broadsheet is twice the size of a page in a tabloid.

WHAT EXAMINERS ARE LOOKING FOR
It is important to understand the different contents and appearance of tabloid and broadsheet newspapers. The task asks you to make a detailed comparison of the two types of paper. The mark scheme would tell examiners to look for 'clear, detailed understanding of how form and layout are used' for an A grade.

Unit 1.3
Audience and purpose

The unit activity is to compare two articles and how they appeal to the papers' readership (see page 23).

Making a start

In Unit 1.2 we looked at the differences between the front pages of a tabloid and of a broadsheet newspaper. What you need to ask yourself now is: What is the reason for such differences? If we look at the newspapers' target audiences, we can get a good idea of why they present news in the way they do. This unit looks at the content of tabloid and broadsheet newspapers as a whole to try to answer that question.

Newspaper content

Tabloids and broadsheets have some common content, for instance both contain home news and sports coverage. They cover these aspects in very different ways and there are some areas covered in tabloids not covered in broadsheets, and vice versa.

A CROSS-SECTION OF NEWSPAPER CONTENT
The content of tabloids and broadsheets includes:

- home news
- international news
- sport
- the arts
- editorial opinion, readers' letters
- advertising
- cartoons

- human interest
- celebrities
- television
- travel
- horoscopes, advice to readers
- business
- finance
- book reviews
- crosswords and other puzzles
- food and drink
- science and technology.

Activity 1.3a

Working in a group, find one tabloid and one broadsheet newspaper (not a Sunday paper).

1. Check how many pages there are in each.
2. Work out roughly how many pages or parts of a page are devoted to each of the aspects of content listed above. Present your findings to the class as rough percentages, for example:

   The Daily Mirror for Saturday 11 January 2003 contained sixty-four pages, twenty-two of which were devoted to sport, i.e. almost 30%.

Who reads what?

By now you should have gathered several different sets of information on the newspapers you have looked at:

- the different ways in which a tabloid and a broadsheet set out individual news items
- the different ways in which a tabloid and a broadsheet set out their front pages
- the different content covered by a tabloid and a broadsheet
- the relative amounts of space given within a tabloid and a broadsheet to the content they choose to cover.

Activity 1.3b   Using the information gathered from your previous activities, try to work out what sort of readership you would expect to find for:

a) the tabloid coverage you have looked at
b) the broadsheet coverage you have looked at.

Hints

- In assessing which kinds of people might prefer to buy a tabloid newspaper, you might ask yourself who would want to buy a newspaper that has:

  - a strong focus on the visual?
  - headlines in very large type?
  - very little text?
  - very limited focus on front page?
  - a lot of sports coverage?
  - sexually suggestive pictures?

- And who would prefer to buy a newspaper that has:

  - a fair focus on visual interest?
  - prominent headlines but not ones that overwhelm everything else?
  - a strong focus on text?
  - a variety of focus on front page?
  - very little about the details of the lives of celebrities?

There are no definitive answers to these questions. There are, after all, lots of people who buy both tabloid and broadsheet newspapers and there are many reasons why people buy newspapers.

Activity 1.3c   In your group, compile a list of reasons why people might buy newspapers. Copy and complete the table.

Reasons why people buy	
tabloid newspapers	broadsheet newspapers
1 To get sports coverage	To get international news
2 To read about celebrities	To read book reviews

You should find that there is a match between the reasons why people buy newspapers and the kind of paper they buy, for example:

- If you have found that your tabloid newspaper devotes a lot of space to sports, including racing tips and racing results, then that is telling you something about the audience for that newspaper.
- If you have found that your broadsheet newspaper devotes a lot of space to international news, then that tells you something about the audience for that newspaper.

Extract
A

Australian Open

Agassi survives the French rapier

Andre Agassi has to stretch for a backhand against Nicolas Escudé – but the Frenchman was chasing shadows at the end

American No2 seed shows title form in duel with livewire

Stephen Bierley
at Melbourne Park

Escudé

There are many exceptionally talented players in the world capable of playing incredible matches, and Andre Agassi knew well that there was danger lurking in the lean and hungry shape of Nicolas Escudé. For it was in this stadium in 2001, on a specially laid grass court, that the Frenchman stunned the Australians by defeating Lleyton Hewitt in the final of the Davis Cup, thereby setting up a shock victory for France.

"You stick a competitor's heart and mind in a guy that has potential, and anything can happen," said Agassi, who knew he had to dampen Escudé's competitive edge as quickly as possible to prevent the Frenchman from igniting and burning through his own defences. Agassi succeeded, winning 6-2, 3-6, 6-3, 6-4 to reach tomorrow's fourth round, but there were anxious moments in the third set for the No2 seed which his next opponent, the 21-year-old Argentinian Guillermo Coria, will have noted.

Coria was suspended at this time last year having failed a drugs test, although he argued that the drug entered his body in a food supplement. His 7-5, 6-2, 6-2 victory over Finland's Jarkko Nieminen put him into the last 16 of a grand slam for the first time. "He's very quick, and if you give someone like that a chance to play his shots he can be pretty dangerous," said Agassi.

This was certainly so in Escudé's case. If anything, he tried to go for a fraction too many winners, and Agassi demonstrated again what a fine defensive player he can be. Escudé was a semi-finalist here in 1998, when he was 21. He has never gone as far in a slam since, and these days is likely to cause the occasional big upset rather than challenge for major honours.

In the third set Escudé had point after point to ram home an advantage based on a whipped double-fisted backhand of ferocious power, coupled with complete dominance at the net. "That third set was pretty fortunate for me all the way around. He's the sort of player that lives and dies by the sword," said Agassi. "It's a risky play, and you just have to hope that he's going to miss more than he gets in." So it proved.

Agassi, a triple champion here, is in the easier half of the draw, hence the growing feeling that an eighth grand slam title is in his grasp at the ripe old age of 32. Against that, he has now gone six slams without a title, and some doubt he can last a fortnight of such intense competition.

Agassi said: "I definitely enjoy winning more now. What makes a difference in the slams is having a good day when you need it, and getting through a tough day when things might not feel that well. Right now I feel real good."

It was certainly a tough day for the No4 seed, Juan Carlos Ferrero of Spain, who took five sets to defeat France's Fabrice Santoro, that frustrating purveyor of the unorthodox. Two other five-set winners were Felix Mantilla, who beat the French Open champion Albert Costa, and South Africa's Wayne Ferreira, 31, who came from two sets down against the American Mardy Fish.

With Goran Ivanisevic poised to return to the circuit after a shoulder operation, Croatia appears to have another future grand slam champion in the 18-year-old Mario Ancic, who is coached by the Dutchman Sven Groeneveld, who formerly worked with Greg Rusedski.

Ancic, who beat Roger Federer at Wimbledon last year, reached the last 32 in only his third slam with a 2-6, 7-6, 6-4, 6-2 win over the Australian wild card Peter Luczac. But the most unlikely player to reach the fourth round was Sargis Sargsian, who knocked out Mark Philippoussis, returning after injury.

from The Guardian,
18 January 2003

Darren LEWIS

From the brink of stardom to the Blackburn scrap-heap, David Dunn is this morning examining the wreckage of his Ewood Park career.

Last summer Sven Goran Eriksson wrestled with the vexed question of whether the north-western wonder could be the answer to his left-sided problem at the World Cup.

Yesterday Rovers boss Graeme Souness washed his hands of the 23-year-old he claims has slipped from promising play-maker to errant playboy.

And anyone who wants the England Under-21 captain, rated at £10 million last summer, can now have him at around half that price, such is Souness's willingness to get him off the Blackburn books.

Dunn has struggled to find his form this season following romances with glamour model Jakki Degg and Emmerdale actress Sam Winward.

Matters cannot have been helped by showbiz gossip last year claiming Degg had been seeing R&B singer Corrie Richards behind his back.

Dunn finally split from Degg earlier this season after she was pictured dancing with Royle Family star Ralf Little in London club Chinawhite.

Kicked out for being a playboy

SOUNESS FED UP WITH PARTY ANIMAL DUNN

MIRROR SPORT broke the news yesterday that Blackburn Rovers were ready to listen to offers for £6-million-rated David Dunn

Anchor

Souness believes that Dunn's tangled love life has contrived to anchor him in a sea of mediocrity during a campaign in which his team-mates have surged towards the brink of retaining the Worthington Cup and stabilised the club's position in the Premiership.

OVER AND DUNN WITH Page 3 model Jakki Degg split up with Dunn last year

Dunn is devastated at that shock assessment – and the manner in which it has been made public – but his manager has no regrets and is sticking to his guns.

Souness said last night: "It's been a disappointing season for David and he has not come anywhere near his standards.

"I have been frustrated with him because clearly there are other things going on in his life that have made him take his eye off the ball.

"That's not something I am prepared to accept because I know he is a better player than he has shown me this year.

"Maybe at this stage in his career, David needs someone else to be talking to him and telling him different things.

"We would be reluctant sellers, but I have already met with his agent and expressed my opinion that if we got an offer we would listen to what they had to say."

Dunn is an outstanding all-rounder, who could have been a cricketer or a rugby league player had he not gone into football.

An ambassador and an example to England's young guns at the Under-21 European Championship in Switzerland last year, Dunn impressed everyone around him with his conduct, his ability and his handling of the media.

Dunn's off-field lifestyle sees him featured in the current issue of Loaded

Yet Souness is known to be irritated that the player's hero is Paul Gascoigne – a man whose stellar abilities crumbled to dust because of his lack of football focus.

Newspaper pictures of Dunn at London parties with topless models and magazine features linking him with alcohol have also angered the Blackburn manager.

Dunn met Degg, from whom he split last autumn, in a London nightclub.

He even revealed he was on his way to the capital to see her when he received his England call-up from Eriksson on his mobile phone.

continued on page 22

continued from page 21

Fashion

The pair were snapped canoodling at the appropriately named Shhh nightclub in London's Leicester Square last February.

They were also pictured together at a celebrity fashion show – in which Dunn took to the catwalk – at Manchester's Palace Hotel two months later.

His appearance was for charity, however, and Dunn has always insisted that his nights out have never sunk into excess.

Indeed, in this month's edition of lad's magazine *Loaded*, he also hit out at claims that he is not pulling his weight as Rovers go from strength to strength this season.

He said: "No matter how well you're playing you always get someone who reckons you are not trying hard enough.

"But on the other hand the majority of supporters have been great since I have been in the first team.

"They have been right behind me.

"Old players go on about how much they used to get p****d the night before a match.

"I like to go out and have a drink but if you were drinking every night these days it would catch up with you. With the pace of this game especially, you'd be knackered and would probably end up puking all over the pitch."

The row is all a far cry from last year's European Championship campaign.

Then the Under-21 boss, David Platt, regularly fired off rave reviews to Eriksson about his midfield general.

Such was the esteem in which Dunn was held, Eriksson had him on standby for his World Cup squad in Japan and South Korea in the event of any injuries.

Dunn was even picked for the England squad on his own merits after the World Cup had come and gone.

Now, however, he is sidelined with a torn calf muscle and is not expected to play again for at least two weeks.

But that will be nothing to the broken heart he will be suffering at the latest blow to his young career.

from Daily Mirror, *11 January 2003*

However, it is important to avoid stereotyping the readers of newspapers. So do not make too many assumptions – people are complex. A person may buy one paper for its coverage of sport and another for its coverage of international news. It tends to be assumed that tabloid newspapers are exclusively read by working-class people and broadsheets exclusively by middle-class people. Although there is broadly some truth in that, the reality is not so simple.

Interest is the key – people buy newspapers because they are interested in what is in them. If you have many interests, you may buy more than one newspaper. If you are highly educated, you may buy a tabloid which does not require extensive reading skills, but if you are poorly educated it is unlikely you will buy a broadsheet that requires better reading skills than you possess.

Identifying the audience

Look at Extracts A and B. If we consider the headlines, the pictures and introductory sentences, we can get some idea of what the audience for these two articles might be.

The headlines

The two headlines are very different. The broadsheet's 'Agassi survives the French rapier' is in formal English and speaks metaphorically of the French player's tennis racquet as a rapier (a type of sword), suggesting his speed, skill and danger as an opponent. The tabloid's headline 'Kicked out for being a playboy' is in colloquial English and, despite the passing reference to football in 'kicked out', it is about the player's playboy lifestyle rather than about football.

The accompanying pictures

Both main pictures are action shots of the players but the tabloid's picture has an inset smaller picture of 'Dunn's off-field lifestyle' as well as, below the article, a picture of his ex-girlfriend naked.

Introductory sentences

The emboldened opening sentence of the tabloid article focuses on emotion and extremes: 'stardom' and 'scrapheap'. *The Guardian's* introductory sentence summarises the content as an account of a match between Agassi and Escudé, taking up the rapier metaphor to describe it as a duel.

Audience and circulation

The circulation figures (how many people buy a particular newspaper) reinforce the fact that the vast majority of people prefer to read newspapers that are published in tabloid form and have more pictures than text. Quite a small percentage of the population reads broadsheet newspapers.

The evidence of the two newspaper articles suggests that most people are more attracted to articles about people's private lives, especially their sex lives, than to the work they do which is the reason for their celebrity. Colloquial and clichéd language is preferred to standard English and more complex metaphor.

Although we need to bear in mind that a good many of the people who buy broadsheet newspapers also at times buy tabloids, it is difficult to escape the conclusion that the broadsheet readers are those with a high standard of reading skills. Since they form a relatively small proportion of the population, the newspapers they read have smaller circulations.

NEWSPAPER CIRCULATION
You can deduce a good deal from a newspaper's circulation figures:

- *The Sun* – 3,507,176
- *Daily Mirror* – 2,220,996
- *Daily Express* – 959,464
- *News of the World* – 4,042,714 (Sunday newspaper)
- *The Guardian* – 414,425
- *The Times* – 717,657
- *The Daily Telegraph* – 1,023,510
- *The Independent* – 230,453.

WHAT EXAMINERS ARE LOOKING FOR
For GCSE English it is very important to identify the intended audience for any piece of text and to understand the writer's purposes. The mark scheme will contain 'content descriptors' which will say, for example, that a tabloid article is 'not very serious', while a broadsheet article on the same subject 'aims to give the whole story'.

Serious practice

UNIT ACTIVITY 1.3 Choose two articles on the same subject, one from a tabloid and one from a broadsheet.

1 Assess the ways in which they are different.
2 How do these differences make them appealing to different readers?

Unit 1.4
The language of newspapers

The unit activity is to compare the language of tabloid and broadsheet newspapers (see page 29).

Making a start

The language of newspapers is different from the language used anywhere else. It is very easy to identify, particularly when it comes to the language of headlines. So what is it that makes it so distinctive?

The language of headlines

You will have noticed from the work you have done in previous units that tabloid headlines are often different from headlines in broadsheet newspapers. Look at the examples of newspaper headlines below, which come from a range of different newspapers.

1 **DIDDLY SQUAT**
UN inspectors find NOTHING in Iraq

2 **Our culture of convenience**

3 **JESSIE, YOU'RE A MESSIE!**

4 **The growing debt for graduates**

5 **LAGER THAN LIFE**

6 **£9,000 A WEEK TO PAY FOR ONE ASYLUM SEEKER**

7 **US begins secret talks to secure Iraq's oilfields**

8 **Police raids aim to smash Turkish mafia**

9 **Mobile bills to be cut**

10 **More tiers for students in Clarke shake-up**

Activity 1.4a   In a group, discuss which headlines you think might belong to each of these newspapers:

- *Daily Express*
- *The Guardian*
- *Daily Mirror*
- *The Daily Telegraph.*

(You will find the answers on page 29.)

What did you find?

You probably found it easy to identify some of the headlines as belonging to a tabloid or a broadsheet, but it is not always simple to differentiate them and it is not easy to know which tabloid or which broadsheet would use any given headline unless it expresses a clear political viewpoint.

- 'Diddly squat' and 'Jessie you're a messie' are immediately recognisable as tabloid headlines because the former uses an extreme kind of slang and the latter has a very personal feel to it as well as changing the word 'messy' to make it look almost identical to 'Jessie'. These techniques are rarely used by broadsheet newspapers although, as we shall see, they also play with language.
- 'US begins secret talks to secure Iraq's oilfields' is likely to be from a broadsheet newspaper because it is in standard English and, although it is related to a very emotive topic, the possible war between Iraq and the US, the words used are in a formal **register** and are in no way sensational.
- 'Police raids aim to smash Turkish mafia' is a tabloid headline. The emotive words 'smash' and 'mafia' are typical **journalese** and could be found in either tabloids or broadsheets.
- 'Our culture of convenience', which you might expect with its **Latinate** words to be from a broadsheet, is from the *Daily Express*. It is not very different in language or tone from the *The Guardian*'s 'The growing debt for graduates'. Both use standard English and words which in themselves are not highly emotive.
- 'Lager than life' uses a play on words that is recognisably in **tabloidese**, while '£9,000 a week to pay for one asylum seeker' has the simple emotional appeal we might expect from a tabloid.

Distinctive features of headlines

We have seen that headlines use a variety of language, with the tabloids tending to be more reliant on slang and colloquialisms, while the broadsheets use more formal English. We have also noted that words are used in a way we do not normally use them in everyday life. There are other distinctive features of headlines. They:

- often substitute one word class for another, so that something we think of as a noun is used as an adjective
- omit most of the joining words such as 'but' or 'and'
- omit articles such as 'the' or 'an' and linking pronouns such as 'who' or 'which'
- are often ambiguous because of these omissions
- often use puns or plays on words
- do not use much punctuation
- create hyphenated words such as 'drug-fuelled', 'love-tug'
- abbreviate words, such as 'teen' for 'teenager'.

The following headlines are all ambiguous in one way or another:

USEFUL WORDS

journalese
The kind of language used by newspapers in general. The words used are often normal words but they are used differently from our normal usage. For instance, headlines often use words like 'bid for' or 'crash' in ways we would never use them in speech or other types of writing. Sometimes they are words used nowhere else except in newspapers.

tabloidese
The language of tabloid newspapers. Phrases like 'bid for' are part of this, but this kind of language is much more extensive in tabloid newspapers where anyone's argument against something they disagree with is a 'protest', any child of parents who are in disagreement is a 'love-tug child' and any fire is a 'blaze'.

register
The degree of formality of language used – it defines how different kinds of language *register* in your mind, how you become aware of them. So broadsheet newspapers use more formal language, standard English, while tabloids use more colloquial language and slang.

Latinate
Derived from the Latin language. For instance, 'culture' derives from the Latin *cultura* which means growing or cultivation.

genre
A kind or type of writing. Newspaper writing is a genre, just as poetry and drama are genres. Headline writing is a sub-genre, or offshoot, of newspaper writing generally.

lexis
Another word that means words or vocabulary.

'Allies push bottles up Germans' was a famous Second World War headline. The main cause of ambiguity here is the use of 'push'. It is intended to be read as a noun so that 'allies push' is the subject of the sentence, which would be clearer if there were an apostrophe after 'allies'. However we tend to read it so that 'allies' is the subject, 'push' the verb and 'bottles' the object, creating a very humorous effect.

Activity 1.4b

1 Work out what makes the other three headlines ambiguous.
2 Find some other examples of ambiguous headlines from your current reading of newspapers.

The language of newspaper articles

There are similarities in the kinds of words newspapers use in headlines and in the text of articles, although headlines are a sub-genre of their own for the reasons shown above. To find out what kind of language is typical of the newspaper genre we need to look at examples.

Extract A

BLOODBATH PLOTTED IN SLUM

Gang lair is derelict farmhouse

By **MIKE SULLIVAN, crime editor** and **JUSTIN PENROSE**

FIVE men suspected of plotting a London bomb bloodbath were arrested in a crumbling farmhouse slum.

The gang of Moroccans were seized by Italian cops who raided a squalid, damp-ridden hovel in a yard filled with junk.

The abandoned farm, with plaster missing from walls and rotten shutters gaping open at windows, had been used as a planning HQ by the mob.

Cops found a cache of deadly C4 explosive, maps of central London and details of potential targets including a Nato military base in Italy.

Incongruously, two pushbikes were propped up outside the house – which was strewn with empty beer cans despite Islamic laws banning alcohol.

Yesterday the five were being held for questioning following Wednesday's dramatic swoop in Badia Polesin, 40 miles south of Venice.

Only two could speak any Italian and interpreters were being brought in for the other three, but all five denied knowing the explosive was there.

from The Sun, 24 January 2003

Extract A is part of a report of the arrest of five Moroccans believed to have links to Al-Qa'ida. The main headline was large enough to fill about a third of the tabloid page.

This is an excellent example of the tabloid style of writing. We can analyse it by looking at the choice of **lexis** with particular attention to the:

- choice and use of adjectives
- choice of nouns
- choice of verbs
- length and structure of sentences
- paragraphing.

Choice and use of adjectives

Some of the obvious adjectives in Extract A are 'crumbling', 'squalid', 'damp-ridden', 'rotten', 'deadly', 'abandoned'. Adjectives can broadly be put into three categories:

- words which are neutral, i.e. they do not have any obvious emotional content
- words which are emotive in a way that is negative or unpleasant
- words which are emotive in a way that is positive or appealing.

All the words in the list above fit into the second category – they are all negative emotive words. Clearly then *The Sun* writers have set out to appeal to their readers' emotions, not to give them a factual story. The combination of words that describe the sordid nature of the place where the men were found and words suggestive of the evil nature of their actions produce quite a powerful effect. They are all words of an extreme nature.

Note also the use of 'damp-ridden', an adjective created by putting together the noun 'damp' and the past participle 'ridden'. Tabloid newspapers are fond of using hyphenated adjectives to build up emotive effect.

Choice of nouns

The headline displays an interesting choice of nouns. Its power derives partly from the structure, which sets the two nouns 'bloodbath' and 'slum' either side of the emotive verb 'plotted'. 'Bloodbath' sets the reader thinking of the worst possible results of the activities going on in the farmhouse, while 'slum' puts the worst possible connotations on the environment in which the men were found. By associating the men with seedy and rotten surroundings, the surroundings become a symbol of what the newspaper thinks of suspected terrorists. By envisaging the carnage that could result from their actions, the newspaper hopes to enlist their readers on their side in the debate.

An emotive effect is also created through the combination of the three nouns 'London', 'bomb' and 'bloodbath' in the phrase 'London bomb bloodbath', where effectively 'London' and 'bomb' become adjectival. Also the word 'bloodbath' itself has been made by taking the noun 'blood' and connecting it to the noun 'bath' in such a way that it has the function of an adjective. The five men are described as a 'gang', which immediately suggests criminal activity, while the police are 'cops', which gives the feel of a sensational television movie.

Activity 1.4c

1 Copy the table. In pairs, discuss and decide which category the following words belong to. Decide whether each word is a noun, verb or adjective.

Word	Neutral	Emotional and negative	Emotional and positive	Noun, verb or adjective

ace	crucial	interest	ratings
battling	dodgy	man-eater	rebel
bigger	feud	nails	scrap
blow	good-as-gold	ordeal	sensational
broke	grilled	ousted	shock
consecutive	heartache	outlawed	sleaze
cops	humiliated	plea	thug

2 Make a list of some of the verbs used by the writers in Extract A. Analyse them along the same lines as the nouns and adjectives. Are they emotive? What effect does the newspaper hope to create by their choice?

Length and structure of sentences

The sentences are fairly short but most include a subordinate clause such as 'who raided a squalid damp-ridden hovel in a yard filled with junk'. The last sentence has two clauses after the opening one, one introduced by 'and' and one by 'but'. So the sentences are long enough to give a powerful effect without being too complex for readers who do not want to, or cannot, cope with complex English. The emphasis is on monosyllables: 'bomb' and 'slum' for instance, although there is some more difficult vocabulary, such as 'incongruously'.

Paragraphing

The paragraphs are all short so they hold the interest of the reader more easily. Each paragraph contains a single focus: the arrest of suspected terrorists, the place in which they were found, and so on.

Extract B is a response to the announcement that students will have to pay back much increased fees from 2006.

Extract B

Anger over student debt burden

Will Woodward
Education editor

The government was last night braced for vigorous protests inside and outside parliament as student leaders warned that the most radical shake-up of higher education since the 60s, unveiled yesterday, will leave new graduates with debts of £30,000.

The promise of grants of £1,000 for the poorest students and the end of up-front tuition fees barely sweetened the bitter pill offered by the education secretary, Charles Clarke, as he confirmed plans to charge English students up to £3,000 a year in fees from 2006, payable after graduation.

Though some of the 150 Labour MPs who signed motions opposing top-up fees appeared to have been assuaged, most, including many loyalists, regarded the statement as a betrayal of Labour's manifesto commitment not to introduce top-up fees. Such anger could trigger the largest backbench revolt this parliament. The Conservatives and Liberal Democrats also opposed the plans.

from The Guardian, *23 January 2003*

Activity 1.4d   Analyse the writer's choice of adjectives, verbs and nouns in Extract B, in the same way as for Extract A.

Sentence structure and paragraphing

The sentences in Extract B are much more complex, longer and more grammatically involved than in Extract A. Like the tabloid, the broadsheet sticks to a main point per paragraph, but the paragraphs are longer because of the greater complexity of the sentences.

Use of imagery

The Guardian makes use of metaphor in 'unveiled' and 'sweetened the bitter pill'. *The Sun* relies on visual imagery, although some of the individual journalese words are themselves metaphoric, for example, 'bloodbath' and 'swoop'.

Tone

It is important to be aware of the tone of voice the journalist uses. The tone used reveals the point of view, which in turn is often related to the newspaper's political bias.

We have been looking at tone already in assessing the emotive nature of the words used in Extracts A and B.

- *The Sun's* tone is passionate and its attitude clearly biased. It does not leave open any possibility that the men concerned might not be guilty. There is scorn in the description of the 'damp-ridden hovel'.
- *The Guardian's* bias is less obvious and the tone is more simply informative than that of *The Sun*. The most emotive word used, 'betrayal', is not given as expressing the newspaper's opinion but is attributed to Labour rebels. However, choosing to write the article from the point of view of the anger it will provoke suggests that the paper is broadly sympathetic to opponents of the new policy and it seems to accept the policy as a 'bitter pill'.

Serious practice

UNIT ACTIVITY 1.4   1 Choose two articles, one from a tabloid and one from a broadsheet newspaper and analyse them in a similar way.
2 When you have compiled your material, write a comparison of the ways in which the two newspapers choose and use words, sentences and paragraphs.

WHAT EXAMINERS ARE LOOKING FOR
It is vital to be able to write about the language writers use in whatever kind of text you are studying. You also need to be able to use the 'jargon' such as that given in this unit. The mark scheme will ask for 'a clear explanation of text' and 'some appropriate terminology' for a C grade.

Answers to Activity 1.4a:

1 *Daily Mirror*, 10/01/03; 2 *Daily Express*, 23/01/03; 3 *Daily Mirror*, 10/01/03; 4 *The Daily Telegraph*, 23/01/03; 5 *Daily Mirror*, 23/01/03; 6 *Daily Express*, 23/01/03; 7 *The Guardian*, 23/01/03; 8 *The Guardian*, 23/01/03; 9 *Daily Express*, 23/01/03; 10 *The Daily Telegraph*, 23/01/03.

Unit 1.5

Non-fiction: structure, language and purpose

The unit activity is to compare two extracts in terms of structure, language and purpose (see page 35).

Making a start

We have looked briefly at the range of topics found in newspapers and at the amount of coverage tabloids and broadsheets give to them. Non-fiction texts also cover a wide range of different areas and ways of presenting them.
The main difference is that the many types of text are not collected together as they are in a newspaper.

This unit will look at some of those non-fiction texts, their structure, choice of language and their purpose. By the end of the unit you should understand the distinctive features of leaflets and reference material and be able to make comparisons between different types of non-fiction text.

Leaflets

These days we are bombarded with leaflets from all sorts of organisations. They are to be found in doctors' waiting rooms, clinics, post offices and shops, and they make up a considerable proportion of our junk mail. To have any effect on a jaded public, they have to be visually effective and easy to read.

Part of Unit Activity 1.1 was to look at an article from an encyclopaedia and at part of a leaflet attempting to persuade people not to use disposable nappies. There you were looking for obvious differences between the two. You will therefore have noted some of the obvious features of the leaflet, including:

* more pictures than text
* a varied layout that mixes text and pictures to provide visual stimulus
* cartoon-type pictures
* a series of pictures in circles to highlight points also made in text
* exclamatory headings to attract attention
* a variety of fonts
* some use of colour.

The visual impact of a leaflet

How do the designers of leaflets try to make us take an interest in something that we have not asked for? Most importantly, they have to seduce us through the appearance of the leaflet. The nappy leaflet in Unit 1.1 (pages 10–11) has a variety of visual features:

* cartoon-type pictures, appealing often through humour
* pictures suggestive of movement and action
* a series of pictures along the bottom of the leaflet highlighting good reasons for using real nappies
* pictures that show ordinary aspects of our domestic life
* pictures that appeal to our imagination.

Some of the pictures illustrate two or more of these features. For instance, the nappy mountain on the top left is humorous. It may remind us of other EU 'mountains' such as the 'butter mountain' or the 'wine mountain'. Its humour is also increased by the tiny figure of a baby in a nappy with an exclamation mark over its head. The baby is bewildered by the way adult human beings organise things (or fail to do so!). Although the picture is humorous, it also has a serious effect in helping us to visualise the fantastic number of disposable nappies to be dealt with by local authorities every year.

Every leaflet is different

Of course, since leaflets are used for so many different purposes, they are all going to be different. Extract A is the inside of a leaflet about how to ensure that you fit safe car seats for children.

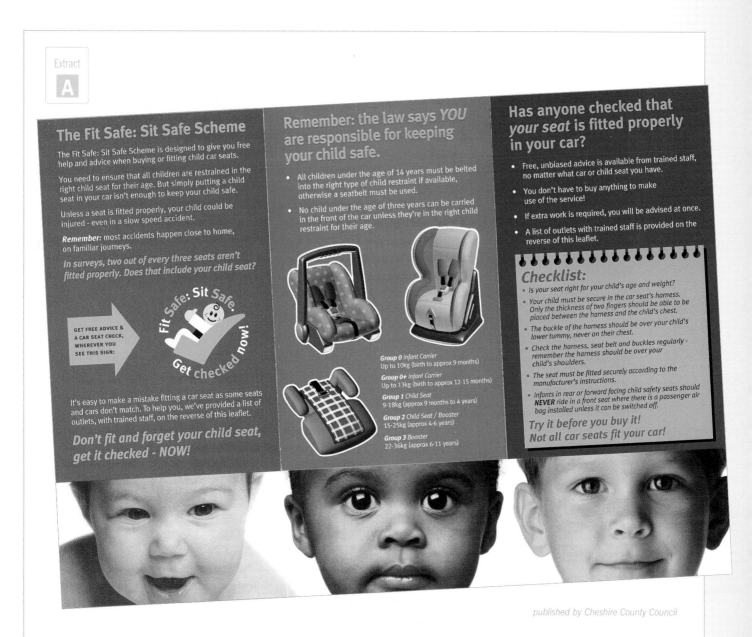

Extract

A

The Fit Safe: Sit Safe Scheme

The Fit Safe: Sit Safe Scheme is designed to give you free help and advice when buying or fitting child car seats.

You need to ensure that all children are restrained in the right child seat for their age. But simply putting a child seat in your car isn't enough to keep your child safe.

Unless a seat is fitted properly, your child could be injured - even in a slow speed accident.

Remember: most accidents happen close to home, on familiar journeys.

In surveys, two out of every three seats aren't fitted properly. Does that include your child seat?

GET FREE ADVICE & A CAR SEAT CHECK, WHEREVER YOU SEE THIS SIGN!

Fit Safe: Sit Safe. Get checked now!

It's easy to make a mistake fitting a car seat as some seats and cars don't match. To help you, we've provided a list of outlets, with trained staff, on the reverse of this leaflet.

Don't fit and forget your child seat, get it checked - NOW!

Remember: the law says YOU are responsible for keeping your child safe.

- All children under the age of 14 years must be belted into the right type of child restraint if available, otherwise a seatbelt must be used.
- No child under the age of three years can be carried in the front of the car unless they're in the right child restraint for their age.

Group 0 *Infant Carrier*
Up to 10kg (birth to approx 9 months)

Group 0+ *Infant Carrier*
Up to 13kg (birth to approx 12-15 months)

Group 1 *Child Seat*
9-18kg (approx 9 months to 4 years)

Group 2 *Child Seat / Booster*
15-25kg (approx 4-6 years)

Group 3 *Booster*
22-36kg (approx 6-11 years)

Has anyone checked that your seat is fitted properly in your car?

- Free, unbiased advice is available from trained staff, no matter what car or child seat you have.
- You don't have to buy anything to make use of the service!
- If extra work is required, you will be advised at once.
- A list of outlets with trained staff is provided on the reverse of this leaflet.

Checklist:

- Is your seat right for your child's age and weight?
- Your child must be secure in the car seat's harness. Only the thickness of two fingers should be able to be placed between the harness and the child's chest.
- The buckle of the harness should be over your child's lower tummy, never on their chest.
- Check the harness, seat belt and buckles regularly - remember the harness should be over your child's shoulders.
- The seat must be fitted securely according to the manufacturer's instructions.
- Infants in rear or forward facing child safety seats should **NEVER** ride in a front seat where there is a passenger air bag installed unless it can be switched off.

Try it before you buy it! Not all car seats fit your car!

published by Cheshire County Council

We are now adding to the list of aspects you looked at in the earlier unit. Here we shall be looking at the targeted audience for the leaflet and at the text to assess its impact on the target audience. This leaflet is published by a local authority to advertise the existence of Child In-Car Care Centres. This is part of their 'Safety on the Move' campaign to persuade the public to take more measures to ensure the safety of themselves and their families when travelling.

'The public' is a very general target. When you have looked at the text and layout of the leaflet you should be able to judge whether it is likely to appeal to a very wide audience.

The text

Before doing the first activity, look at the section of text in Extract A with the heading 'Remember: the law says YOU are responsible for keeping your child safe' and the two bullet points below it. Look at the kind of language used and consider the kind of audience it might appeal to:

- **How many sentences are there in this piece of text?** There are two sentences.
- **Are the sentences simply constructed?** The first bullet point has 26 words in it and the second 27. Both sentences are clearly written and relatively simple, consisting of one main clause and one subordinate clause.
- **Do they use mostly monosyllables or polysyllables?** Both sentences contain a mixture of monosyllables and polysyllables. The polysyllabic words tend to be Latinate, words like 'restraint' and 'available'. They are not particularly difficult words, but they are not the kind of words used by the section of society that has little interest in reading for its own sake.
- **What sort of audience do you think this would appeal to?** It would probably appeal mainly to a middle-class audience. The lexis is not simple and full of impact. If that is the case, then the leaflet might not achieve very much because so many middle-class people already go to great trouble to ensure the safety of their children in cars.

You might not agree with this analysis.

Activity 1.5a	Study Extract A, looking at the following aspects.
	1 **The layout of the leaflet**: What is the relationship between headings and text?
	2 **The sections of text**: Are they well chosen and sensibly ordered?
	3 **The kind of language used**: What are its characteristics? Is it simple, complex, Latinate? Is it formal, informal, slangy? Serious or humorous?
	4 **The pictures**: What do the pictures achieve?
	5 **The colour**: Is it effective?

Commercial leaflets

Despite their differences, Extract A and the leaflet in Unit 1.1 are similar in a number of ways. They were both local authority leaflets designed to make our lives safer or more environmentally-friendly. Many leaflets, however, are designed to make businesses more effective and appealing and therefore to increase their cash flow. Extract B is one of that type.

from HSBC plc

*published by
Cheshire County Council*

Apart from the different purpose of Extract B, there are some other notable differences:

- Like all high-profile national firms, HSBC has a very well-known logo and slogan.
- HSBC is also able to use images, such as the house, in a variety of leaflets and in banks so that they become part of the public consciousness.

When comparing Extracts A and B, it is worth bearing in mind that local authorities have a very limited amount of money to spend on a vast range of essential public services, while the big five banks have very much greater resources.

The immediate impact

The immediate impact of a leaflet comes, of course, from its front cover. In the case of Extract B, the leaflet has a bright, deceptively simple cover where red on white makes an impact. The advice to 'Relax – you're in safe hands' is designed to reassure the reader of the stability and the caring nature of the bank. The central image reinforces the words in a humorously literal way.

The leaflet is actually about mortgage cover from the bank. Although it does not say so in words on the front, the picture of the house being cared for shows the content visually. The personification of the house as a smiling person further stresses the happy effect of trusting HSBC. The only other feature on the front is the HSBC slogan and logo. 'The world's local bank' is a clever use of words to suggest both the availability and benefits of a local firm and the power and influence of a worldwide organisation.

Activity 1.5b	Extract C shows the front cover of the leaflet in Extract A.
	Compare it with Extract B. Which do you think is more effective in appealing to its target audience?

Both target audiences are wide. Nearly everyone has a car and many people are careless about safety for their children. Almost the whole population has a bank account and most people own or aspire to owning a property.

Other non-fiction texts

When you looked at the article on cocoa butter from the *Encyclopaedia Britannica* in Unit 1.1 (page 10), you would have been able sum up its visual appearance very easily. It is just text, no picture, no heading beyond the emboldened entry title, no use of colour and it uses quite a small font.

We will now look at the text of this article to see what kind of language is used and why. We can deduce a good deal from the opening sentence:

cocoa butter, also called THEOBRAMA OIL, pale-yellow, edible vegetable fat obtained from cocoa beans, having a mild chocolate flavour and aroma, and used in the manufacture of chocolate confections, pharmaceutical ointments, and toiletries.

The words used are descriptive. A number of adjectives are used, such as 'pale-yellow', 'edible' and 'mild'. They are not used as they might be in poetry to stimulate our imagination, but simply to build up an accurate picture of the characteristics of cocoa butter. The aim is for scientific accuracy, hence the information that cocoa butter is also called theobrama oil. The vocabulary is Latinate and fairly demanding with 'edible', 'stimulate' and 'pharmaceutical'.

COMPARING TWO TEXTS

When you are comparing pieces of text, bear in mind the ways in which they are :

- similar
- different.

In connection with differences, consider such things as layout, wording, illustrations, headings, fonts.

So, you might point out that the two extracts are similar in that they both give information on particular subjects in an objective, scientific way. You might go on to say that they are different in layout and visual impact: use of colour, headings, fonts and in terms of the space given to them on the page.

Activity 1.5c	1	What, do you think, is the target audience for text of the kind given in the *Encyclopaedia Britannica*?
	2	What are the purposes of such texts?
	3	Are they likely to succeed in attracting their target audience?

Reference texts on the Internet

Encarta, Microsoft's on-line encyclopaedia, can be compared with the book equivalent found in the *Encyclopaedia Britannica*. Extract D is an extract from an article on cloning from *Encarta*.

Extract

D

Cloning

I INTRODUCTION

Cloning, creating a copy of living matter, such as a cell or organism. The copies produced through cloning have identical genetic makeup and are known as clones. Many organisms in nature reproduce by cloning. Scientists use cloning techniques in the laboratory to create copies of cells or organisms with valuable traits. Their work aims to find practical applications for cloning that will produce advances in medicine, biological research, and industry.

II OVERVIEW

Farmers started cloning plants thousands of years ago in simple ways, such as taking a cutting of a plant and letting it root to make another plant. Early farmers also devised breeding techniques to reproduce plants with such characteristics as faster growth, larger seeds, or sweeter fruits. They combined these breeding techniques with cloning to produce many plants with desired traits. These early forms of cloning and breeding were slow and sometimes unpredictable. By the late 20th century scientists developed genetic engineering, in which they manipulate deoxyribonucleic acid (DNA), the genetic material of living things, to more precisely modify a plant's genes. Scientists combine genetic engineering with cloning to quickly and inexpensively produce thousands of plants with a desired characteristic.

from encarta.msn.com

Hint

Read the information on comparing texts on page 34.

Serious practice

UNIT ACTIVITY 1.5

1 Compare the extract from the article on cocoa butter (page 10) with Extract D in this unit, in terms of their:

- visual impact
- use of words
- sentence structures and paragraphing
- overall appeal

2 Which of the two do you think is the most likely to appeal to its target audience? Why?

 WHAT EXAMINERS ARE LOOKING FOR
In this unit, you are asked to compare two non-fiction articles in terms of their visual impact and use of language. For an A grade, the mark scheme asks examiners to look for 'clear, detailed comparison' of the ways writers use language.

Unit 1.6
Advertisements and cartoons

The unit activity is to analyse and compare advertisements and cartoons in tabloid and broadsheet newspapers (see page 41).

Making a start

Advertisements

Advertising makes it possible for newspapers to exist. The amount we pay for our papers would not on its own be enough to pay for the immense task of administering and co-ordinating the printing and publishing of the papers.

The tabloid newspapers have a vast circulation compared to the broadsheets, so they are able to attract a lot of advertising, but the broadsheets are also attractive to advertisers because their readers are, on the whole, wealthier than those of the tabloid newspapers. Some identical advertisements can be found in both broadsheet and tabloid newspapers, but they each have some advertisements that are different from those to be found in the other type of newspaper.

It is interesting to compare circulation figures and the costs of advertising in tabloids and broadsheets. Look at the information below – the lower cost of advertising in *The Sun* reflects its circulation of 3,500,000 compared to *The Daily Telegraph's* 1,000,000. *The Times* only has a circulation of 717,657, but it is such a prestigious paper that it attracts a great deal of advertising.

 THE COST OF ADVERTISING

These are examples of the cost of a full-page colour advertisement in some newspapers:

◆ *Daily Express* – £39,375
◆ *The Sun* – £18,900
◆ *The Daily Telegraph* – £50,750
◆ *The Times* – £38,000.

What is immediately obvious is the immense cost of advertising, which gives us some idea of the returns advertisers expect to get for such large sums of money.

Analysing advertisements

For the GCSE examination media questions, you need to be able to 'read' an advertisement so that you understand:

- the effect of the way it is laid out, for example, the use of different fonts and sizes of type, the way pictures and words complement each other
- why the words are chosen, and their likely effect on the reader
- what kinds of pictures are used – photographic, cartoon, etc. – and what effect they have
- the size of the advertisement and its position in the paper.

WHO ADVERTISES WHAT?

The edition of *The Sun* published on 24 January 2003 contained advertisements for the following:

- a range of cars
- credit to buy cars if you have been refused it elsewhere
- DVDs and videos
- seven films
- car services: brakes, batteries, tyres, etc.
- Internet services
- sales, many for furniture stores, flooring specialists/DIY stores
- mobile phones
- home insurance
- Lunn Poly holidays
- Computer World
- many offers of loans, re-mortgages, debt settlement, etc.
- Betfair.

The edition of *The Daily Telegraph* published on 23 January 2003 contained advertisements for these products and services:

- Spanish Rail Cruises, P&O Ferries
- Sharps Bedrooms sale, Magnet sale
- Dollond and Aitchison opticians
- Nationwide mortgages
- Vauxhall, Alfa Romeo, MG and Rover (same advert as in *The Sun*)
- Freeserve
- Scholl flight socks
- Siemens washing machines
- Dell, PCs, speed demon
- AA car insurance
- film – *The Hours*
- Onetel mobiles, T-mobile
- ATS car services
- Richer Sounds sale
- fine wines
- cordless door chime.

Activity 1.6a   Study the two lists above.

1   Which similar products and services are being offered by both tabloid and broadsheet advertising?
2   Which products or services are offered just by the tabloid and which are offered just by the broadsheet?
3   What do you deduce from your findings about the readership of the two types of papers?

Do these factors make a difference?

Overall, you need to be aware of how the advertiser can manipulate you into buying the product. The way in which newspaper advertising works is not very different from the way in which the presentation of the news itself works. Newspaper proprietors and their editorial teams have their own agenda and wish to appeal to their readers in particular ways. They aim to reinforce the prejudices readers already have and to play on their weaknesses.

For that reason, as you have probably discovered in completing Activity 1.6a, the products advertised are chosen because the known audience type for the particular newspaper is likely to be susceptible to particular products. For example, *The Daily Telegraph* advertises fine wines and Alfa Romeos, while *The Sun* advertises Rovers and ways of buying cars when you cannot get credit. Sometimes these advertisements will tell us about the taste of the people concerned, for example, *Telegraph* readers are more likely to enjoy fine wines than *Sun* readers. Sometimes, though, it just tells us about the relative affluence of the people concerned. *Sun* readers would probably like to buy Alfa Romeos, but far fewer of them can afford them than is true of *Telegraph* readers. Many of them cannot afford to buy cars at all, hence the advertisements for credit.

Advert A

Don't forget to join Freeserve, the UK's No.1 ISP.

More people up and down the country are enjoying the freedom of the Internet with Freeserve than any other ISP. And you can join them for just £6.99 a month for your first three months. That's half price. And then it's only £13.99 a month after that. So join the freedom movement, join Freeserve.

from The Sun, 24 January 2003

The immediate impact

Remember that there has to be an immediate impact because few people spend time poring over advertisements. They may, of course, be affected by advertisements in ways they are unaware of, which is one good reason to be able to analyse advertising. The more aware you are of how you are being manipulated, the better able you are to resist it and make your own rational choices.

The first thing you notice in Advert A is the elephant and the number one painted on its side. This, in conjunction with the word *Freeserve,* enables readers to make a connection between the company and the quality suggested by the number one.

The elephant is associated with the phrase 'an elephant never forgets' and the injunction to us in the largest type is 'Don't forget to join Freeserve'.

More subtle aspects

The immediate impact is the only impact the advertisement will have on some readers. However, the details of the picture as a whole must have significance.

If you look more carefully, you can see that the elephant is foregrounded in a museum gallery displaying abstract art. A security man sits looking on in a relaxed way. What is the significance of that? There are probably a number of ways of interpreting it. One possibility is that the elephant represents a large slice of real, moving life and is set against merely decorative, inanimate abstract designs. No one apparently wants to look at them, because the security guard clearly has nothing to do and the elephant is completely ignoring them. The elephant perhaps stands for the action and excitement of surfing the Internet and of finding a source of knowledge such as 'the elephant who never forgets' suggests.

It might strike you as quite surprising that this advertisement, which is far from obvious in some ways, should appear in *The Sun,* which is not noted for its intellectual appeal. However, many modern advertisements are in fact extremely complex and yet seem to have the required effect of selling things even to people who are almost certainly quite unaware of their subtleties.

The text

Advertisements rely much more on pictures than text, but the text is important too. A picture will probably attract the attention initially, drawing the reader to find out what it is advertising. The text in Extract A is simple, stating apparently that Freeserve is used by more people than any other independent service provider. In fact the sentence is ambiguous. It might mean not that more people use Freeserve but that the people who do use it 'enjoy' it unlike other services. The use of the abbreviation ISP shows that people are expected to know what it means. The appeal to the reader is in suggesting that they are excluded if they do not use Freeserve, 'And you can join them' and there is also an appeal to their pocket 'just £6.99 a month', 'That's half price'.

Size

This advertisement takes up a large part of a tabloid page, which must increase its chances of being noticed.

Reading a broadsheet advertisement

from The Daily Telegraph,
23 January 2003

Activity 1.6b   Advert B is an advertisement which took up a quarter of a broadsheet page in *The Daily Telegraph*. Analyse it in the same way as we analysed Advert A above.

Comparing tabloid and broadsheet advertisements

Despite both types of paper carrying some similar advertisements, their advertisements also reflect the different readership.

Cartoons

Some cartoons are very easy to understand at a glance, while others are more obscure and understanding them may depend on how well up in the news you are or on whether you have read the article beside which they are placed.

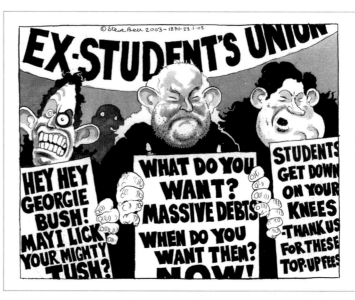

from The Guardian, *23 January 2003*

USEFUL WORDS

cartoon
Cartoons can take various forms but, in the case of a newspaper cartoon, it is a drawing done in a deliberately exaggerated way in order to make people laugh and often it is a form of **satire**.

satire
A way of showing people's stupidities to ridicule them, usually for humorous effect.

WHAT EXAMINERS ARE LOOKING FOR

For a grade A the examiners are looking for an ability to give 'a clear and detailed comparison of how meaning is conveyed in print and image'. For a C grade you need to be able to explain the images and presentational devices used.

Political cartoons

Many cartoons poke fun at politicians. Cartoon A is an example of this type. Some of the aspects you need to notice or be aware of to make sense of cartoons are:

- the setting
- the faces of those being satirised
- the words used
- the news stories on which they are based.

If you examine Cartoon A, you should immediately be able to identify the people being satirised: Tony Blair, Charles Clarke, the Education Minister, and Gordon Brown, the Chancellor of the Exchequer. The setting they are in is the 'Ex-Student's Union'. The three figures are apparently on a demonstration. The setting therefore is not a real one but is part of the joke. It reminds us that these three Labour politicians have all had the benefit going to first-class universities without having to pay fees. Student demonstrations are always protests against the evils of the day, but ironically these three are seen protesting on behalf of their own policies. Blair is satirised as Bush's 'poodle', following US policies slavishly; Clarke, who is responsible for bringing in greatly increased student fees, is protesting in favour of debts, and Gordon Brown is asking to be thanked for the favour the government has done to students!

Cartoons are often highly amusing but they are also a potent weapon in the criticism of government policies. This is quite a hard-hitting cartoon that suggests the government's policy on funding degrees is utterly unacceptable and that the Prime Minister does not have a mind of his own.

Serious practice

Advert C

from The Independent on Sunday,
6 April 2003

from The Sun,
23 January 2003

UNIT ACTIVITY 1.6

1. Study Adverts C and D. Work out why you would expect to find them in the newspapers they appeared in, looking at the same features we have analysed above: layout, size, use of pictures, lexis, and so on.

2. Look at Cartoons B and C, and answer the following questions for each one.

   a) Who is depicted in the cartoon? It may be someone famous or just the man or woman in the street.

   b) What setting are they placed in?

   c) What do you need to know in order to understand the cartoon?

   d) What is the importance of the words used in the cartoon?

   e) What, do you think, is the point being made by the cartoonist?

Cartoon B

"He can't get anything right just now - it's lucky we stopped him making a bit for Safeways."

from The Daily Telegraph,
23 January 2003

Cartoon C

'How much for just the scarf?'

from Daily Mail,
24 January 2003

41

Unit 1.7

Fact and opinion: 1

The unit activity is to analyse two readers' letters (see page 47).

Making a start

Recognising the difference between fact and opinion

It is often difficult to decide what is **fact** and what is not. One of the problems is that writers sometimes present material as though it is factual when it is not.

It can be particularly difficult to decide whether what you read in a newspaper is 'true' or not. All newspapers have their own political affiliations, so you will probably choose which newspaper to buy depending on what your political views are. However, although you might want to have your personal views reflected in the newspaper you read, you also want to know that what you are reading is genuinely 'news', if that is what it is meant to be, and not just the editor's or journalist's **opinion**. For that reason, newspapers have sections where you expect to read what the newspaper's perspective is and other sections where you expect to get a more objective viewpoint.

By the end of the unit you should be able to recognise the difference between fact and opinion in newspapers and be able to analyse the persuasive techniques used by journalists.

Editorial comment

The place where you expect to find the newspaper proprietor's or editor's opinion legitimately presented is in a **leading article**. Leading articles set out the paper's views with no pretence that they are trying simply to present facts. Extract A opposite is an example of a leading article.

FACT OR OPINION?
In looking at Extract A, you need to work out a number of things:

- Which national or international issues are under discussion?
- What are the views being presented?
- How much of the article seems to be factual?
- What techniques does the writer use to express opinions?
- How can you tell that something is opinion rather than fact?

Activity 1.7a

1   Look at Extract A. The two issues under discussion are:

- the possible war against Iraq
- student funding.

Which factor makes it possible for the editor to link them here?

2   When you have established the link, look again at what is said about the government's new plans on student funding. List three or four points which express the editor's view on this new government policy.

How much is factual?

What you have on your list is opinions. To work out what you think is factual, start by looking at each of the opinions you have listed. The following points *might* be described as factual:

- It is certainly true that the government's new plans will leave students with debts of £21,000 or more.

- It is also true that the middle classes, because they pay more taxes than the working class, will effectively be subsidising the university education of poorer students. They will also have to pay more for their own children to go to university.

- Whether the plans will enable students from poorer backgrounds to gain university entrance with inferior qualifications is unclear. There is certainly no evidence here to support it or to suggest, even if it is true that some of these students might have inadequate qualifications, that the same might not be true of middle-class children.

The point that this policy represents a poor deal for British society is *not* a fact.

Extract

Daily Mail

COMMENT

Fighting a war on two fronts

SUDDENLY this most commanding of Prime Ministers looks distinctly vulnerable. No longer is he wielding unchallenged supremacy over New Labour or stamping his authority on the world stage.

At home and abroad, Mr Blair is at bay.

Whatever the rights and wrongs of his support for President Bush over Iraq, his courage is beyond doubt. Labour is bitterly hostile to his policy, while the public is increasingly sceptical. But he sticks to his tough line because he believes it right. And at least he could hope for the backing of key European allies.

Now that hope is blown away. Both Germany – incoming president of the UN Security Council – and the duplicitous French have made it clear they oppose military action against Iraq, in one fell swoop shattering Western unity and raising Saddam Hussein's morale.

Their selfish action raises the disturbing possibility that America will go ahead without a second UN resolution, and expect Britain to join in – a development that would really destroy Labour unity.

And that isn't the end of Mr Blair's worries overseas. In a quite separate development, he has had to reach a humiliating deal with President Chirac to allow Zimbabwe's Robert Mugabe into France, despite the EU's travel ban on that murderous tyrant.

Had Blair not agreed, Chirac would have blocked further sanctions on Zimbabwe. His compliance with this diplomatic chicanery is further evidence of the lameness of his oft-repeated boast that Britain is at the heart of Europe.

And now he is plunged into a potentially devastating crisis at home, over plans to saddle university students with debts of £21,000 or more.

In one move, Mr Blair has succeeded in provoking the fury of his own party and enraging the middle classes, who will not only have to pay more to educate their children, but must subsidise students from poorer backgrounds who under Labour's plans will sail into university with inferior qualifications.

Extra costs to pay for increasingly sub-standard universities ... a poor deal for middle Britain indeed.

Make no mistake. This issue won't go away. No wonder the Prime Minister seems increasingly isolated: A war on two fronts. Never has Mr Blair faced such a huge challenge to win hearts and minds.

Invisible men

IT IS the great black hole at the centre of British politics.

Seldom has the Opposition been presented with so many open goals. Not only is the public deeply uneasy over the asylum shambles, but New Labour is split from top to bottom over university fees.

So where are the Tories? Incredibly, they manage to remain invisible, unheard, ineffective and irrelevant.

This week, Iain Duncan Smith planned a major policy initiative on asylum to tackle Labour's abysmal inability to control our national borders.

So why hasn't his plan seen the light of day, especially as it would undoubtedly have commanded massive support?

Simple. His Home Affairs spokesman Oliver Letwin effectively vetoed it, because he thinks it undermines the Tories' attempts to present themselves as an inclusive, touchy-feely party.

Pathetic! But then, this is part of an all too familiar pattern. Have the Tories uttered a single memorable word in the row over university fees?

Their lack of a killer instinct – indeed their lack of any political instincts at all – is becoming not just embarrassing, but tragic. Their lamentable ineffectiveness and lack of courage leave a yawning gap in politics for extremists to exploit.

Britain needs a proper opposition party.

from Daily Mail, 24 January 2003

How does the writer choose appropriate words to express opinions?

In looking at advertising, you will have seen that the choice of particular words is one of the techniques used to persuade people to buy. Exactly the same applies here. The writer chooses emotive words to persuade readers to adopt the same point of view. If you look at the first sentence dealing with university funding, you will see the emotive words:

> 'And now he is *plunged* into a potentially *devastating crisis* at home, over plans to *saddle* university students with debts of £21,000 *or more.*'

How do these words affect the reader? The verb 'is plunged' suggests violent action and it is a passive verb. It does not tell us that Tony Blair plunged himself into the situation but that some unknown person or force put him into it. That makes it seem as though he is not in control of his own actions. The adjective 'devastating', and the noun 'crisis' which it modifies, are both very emotive words. A crisis is an emergency and if it is devastating it has reached extreme proportions. The verb 'saddle' highlights the view that the new fees are burdensome and will cause discomfort. It might also suggest that in making students pay more, the government is taking away their freedom.

Activity 1.7b	The table lists other emotive words in the article. Copy the table and write down in the right-hand column the effect you think each word might have on readers, and why.

Word	Effect
fury	
enraging	
inferior	
provoking	
sail	

Other techniques used

Sentence structure

As with any piece of writing, we can learn a lot from looking closely at the way sentences are constructed. In the paragraph beginning 'In one move …', there is only one sentence which has a number of clauses. The effect of the subordinate clauses is to build up from the short, decisive 'In one move' through the statement of what Blair has done (again very much a matter of opinion rather than fact), to illustrate through the clauses beginning 'who …', 'but …' and 'who …' the dire results of Blair's actions. To balance this long sentence, there are the dogmatic short sentences: 'Make no mistake. This issue won't go away'.

Tone

Tone is another important tool used by a writer who seeks to persuade. The overall tone of this part of the article is, as often in the writing of leading article, one of implied superiority and wonder that anyone could make the mistakes that politicians do on a regular basis. The word 'succeeded' is used with a tone of sarcasm, since clearly in the writer's opinion Blair has not succeeded at all in the sense we would normally use the word.

Rhetorical devices

There are a lot of other rhetorical devices such as you find in poetry, which are also used by writers of prose. They include rhetorical questions, repetition and alliteration.

Activity 1.7c   Re-read the first part of the article on Blair's attitude to Iraq. Analyse it in the same way as the comment on student funding was analysed above. Look at the choice of lexis, the use of sentences, paragraphing and tone.

Comparing opinion in tabloids

Tabloid opinion and comment sections tend to be similar in many ways from paper to paper. However, there are noticeable differences. To illustrate this, read Extract B from a *Sun* Comment column.

MAKING COMPARISONS

Some of the aspects we can compare in the comment sections from the *Mail* and the *Sun* are:

- the overall headings
- the subheadings
- the layout of paragraphs and the font
- the number of words used
- the choice of words
- the sentence structures
- the tone
- other rhetorical devices
- the audience addressed
- the aims.

Extract B

THE SUN SAYS

Loud voice of the people

THE people have spoken with a loud voice. So when will the politicians listen?

Over 100,000 Sun readers have signed our petition urging the Government to get tough on asylum.

But Tony Blair and David Blunkett seem to be busy doing nothing.

The Prime Minister complains about the anti-war lobby and gears the nation for an attack on Iraq.

But at the same time, terrorists walk free in our own country.

The Home Secretary says society is "like a coiled spring" but fails to address the cause of public anger.

He even has a pop at newspapers and accuses them of writing that we should stop letting families flee to Britain.

That is a grotesque distortion of what the debate is really about.

Genuine need or desire to work is not the issue, as he well knows.

It is the hundreds of thousands of bogus asylum seekers who have vanished among us.

It is the armed Turkish, Albanian and Kosovan drug gangs who pollute our streets.

It is the impossible demands made on the floundering NHS, schools and the welfare system.

It is the terrorists who want to kill us but live on State handouts.

We have lost control of our borders and our country is being snatched away from us.

That's why 100,000 Sun readers are like coiled springs, Home Secretary.

from The Sun, *24 January 2003*

The overall headings

The overall headings are there to tell the reader that this is the section of the paper where editorial opinions are given.

Is there any major difference between '*Daily Mail* Comment' and 'The Sun says'?

*   The *Mail's* use of the word 'comment' seems simply to suggest that this is where we shall find the paper's viewpoint.
*   On the other hand, 'The Sun says' has a different tone. It seems much more dogmatic, as if to tell us that since this is what the paper says, we had better agree with them.

The subheadings

*   The subheading 'Loud voice of the people', which is emphasised by underlining, seems to fit in with the suggested view of the main heading. *The Sun* here appears to see itself as the voice of the people. Their justification for this is that they have organised a petition to try to persuade the government to be much tougher in granting asylum.
*   The *Mail's* 'Fighting a war on two fronts' is much more descriptive, a metaphorical way of saying that Blair not only wants to fight literally in Iraq but that metaphorically he has to fight opponents on that issue and on the issue of student funding. The *Mail's* subheading is more subtle and less strident than the *Sun's*.

Activity 1.7d

1   Make a rough calculation of how many words there are in Extracts A and B. What do you think is suggested by the relative number of words used?
2   Look at the *Sun's* choice of words in Extract B. Are they simple, mainly monosyllabic words, or Latinate, polysyllabic words? How many of them are emotive? Does the article use slang or colloquialisms or is it in formal English?
3   Are the sentences in Extract B short and simple or long and complex? Or are they a mixture of the two? Is there any use of repetition? If so, what effect does it have?
4   What is the overall tone of Extract B?
5   Use the notes you have already made to compare Extracts A and B.

Editorial aims

Whatever differences you have discovered between the two articles should help you to answer the question 'What are the aims of these editorial comments?' Editorial comment may have a number of different aims, including to:

*   sell papers
*   reflect the political opinion of the newspaper proprietor
*   appeal to those people who share the same political viewpoint
*   persuade those who are not yet convinced
*   at election times, to affect the votes cast and the government elected.

So, the editorial comment found in newspapers plays a very important role in national life. Newspapers are powerful political tools and the bigger their circulation, the more powerful they are – *The Sun* has a circulation of 3,500,00; the *Mail* a circulation of 2,500,000.

Activity 1.7e   In a group, discuss whether you think Extract B reflects any or all of the editorial aims suggested above. How have you come to your conclusions?

Opinion in the newspaper as a whole

The leading articles are, of course, by no means the only parts of a paper that reflect particular viewpoints. The letters written by readers, often published alongside the editorial comment, also reflect opinions, in this case the opinions of readers. Whereas in local newspapers you may get letters reflecting a number of different political viewpoints, in national newspapers the letters tend to reflect the editorial view.

The news articles themselves, although theoretically 'informing' the readers, are often deeply and obviously biased. A good example would be 'Bloodbath plotted in slum' in Unit 1.4 (page 26). Even if the article presents a number of facts, it may still be biased in the choice of which facts to present.

There is nothing wrong with bias in itself. We each have an individual bias. The important thing is to be able to work out when we are being given factual information and when we are not and also when we are only being given some of the facts. As long as we can tell the difference, we can make our own minds up as to what we believe.

Serious practice

UNIT ACTIVITY 1.7   1   Read Extracts C and D, which are letters to newspapers.

   a)   Write in your own words what each letter is saying.
   b)   Analyse the ways in which the message is put across in each letter, as shown in this unit.
   c)   Decide whether you think the writer has put the message across effectively in each case.

2   Find two other letters from local or national newspapers and carry out the same analysis as above.

WHAT EXAMINERS ARE LOOKING FOR
The focus here is on distinguishing between fact and opinion. You can gain marks simply by recognising one from the other, but you will get more marks for explaining the difference. The more explanation you can give, the higher your grade is likely to be.

Extract **C**

The number one issue at the next General Election will be asylum seekers and which party is going to stem the tide flooding into Britain.

New Labour has failed to come up with an effective policy and the country's resources are being stretched to the limit. It's time to shut up shop.

Brian Cavendish, Gloucester

letter to The Sun, *25 April 2003*

Extract **D**

The real issue is that 50% of teachers will reach retirement age within 15 years and they are not being replaced in anything like the numbers required to make up a shortfall; teachers' salaries are still over 30% behind their relative position of 20 years ago and to make up that shortfall would require a hike in taxation that the government is not prepared to countenance.

Ian Parsons, Bradford

letter to The Guardian, *25 April 2003*

Unit 1.8

Fact and opinion: 2

The unit activity is to compare a tabloid and a broadsheet leading article in terms of content, language and tone (see page 53).

Making a start

This unit looks in more detail at the presentation of information and how to detect where bias creeps in. It also looks at leading articles where we expect to find the expression of a newspaper's opinion, comparing how opinion is presented in the two types of paper.

Factual writing

Factual writing provides information without any personal opinion attached to it. A good example is Extract A.

Extract **A**

Multiple e-mail users

> **Set up Outlook Express to manage your e-mail for you, create separate e-mail identities and protect the privacy of your messages.**

Outlook Express has a useful feature that allows you to set up a user name and password for every member of the family. These separate 'identities' – as they are known – function like individual letterboxes: each person's mail arrives in his or her own inbox, so there is no chance of getting someone else's post by mistake. This is a very handy feature if several people are using the same computer to collect their messages.

Switching identities

You don't have to make a new Dial-Up Networking connection for each new e-mail account. If you're all on the same ISP, you can switch identities without disconnecting. If the new user has a completely different ISP and account, you can tell Outlook Express to disconnect and reconnect to the new ISP automatically when switching identities.

from How to Do Just About Anything on the Internet *(Reader's Digest)*

Features of language use in Extract A

- There is almost no lexis that indicates a personal opinion. Only the words 'useful' and 'handy' betray the view of the writer, although the information given suggests that the e-mailing system described would be useful. In this case, the vast majority of people would probably agree that the system described would be useful or handy to anyone wanting to use e-mail. They are words that express a calm viewpoint rather than emotions.
- The article is in the **third person** but makes much use of 'you' which makes the passage more personal: 'You don't have to', 'You can', etc.
- It uses a simile, 'like individual letterboxes', but simply for clarification rather than for descriptive effect.
- There are not many adjectives and those used are, like the simile, used to make meaning clear rather than for descriptive effect.

USEFUL WORDS

bias

An inclination to favour one side or another in an argument; a viewpoint that is weighted towards a particular view or person. The word 'bias' can be a noun or a verb. If you favour one side over another you have 'a bias', the word here is a noun; but if you say 'This experience may bias you', 'bias' here is used as a verb. The adjective formed from 'bias' is 'biased'. Candidates frequently write about somebody being 'bias' when what they mean is 'biased'.

prejudice

A preconceived opinion that is not based on a rational consideration of the issues. There is a difference between bias and prejudice therefore.

We all have opinions about a variety of topics.

If we consider the issues before making up our minds, we may be described as biased. If our opinions are based purely on emotion without a consideration of the facts, then we are prejudiced. The word 'prejudice' can be a noun or a verb. The adjective formed from it is 'prejudiced' – note the spelling!

first, second and third person

- If a text is written in the first person, it uses 'I' or 'we' to express the viewpoint of the speaker directly.
- If it is written in the third person, it uses the pronouns 'he', 'she' or ' they', and so the writer is describing the situation, action or events from the outside.
- If it is written in the second person, it uses the pronoun 'you' and addresses the reader directly.

Activity 1.8a

1 Write two or three paragraphs of information about any subject you are knowledgeable about.
2 Write a short commentary on your writing, looking at features of language such as those listed above.

Hints

For instance, you need to comment on the kinds of words chosen. Check whether there are any words in it like 'useful' and 'handy' and say why you have used them. In what way are those kinds of words different from words like 'e-mail' or 'Internet'?

Giving advice

A kind of non-fiction writing that can be very close to factual writing is the giving of tips or advice. How likely advice is to be factual depends to a large extent on the subject on which advice is being offered. Extract B is a list of some of the '50 top tips' given to *Radio Times* readers by the gardening expert Alan Titchmarsh.

Extract B

PLANNING

1 Don't do anything to a new garden before living with it for at least three months. That way, you can work out where the sunniest spot for the patio is, for example, and what you really need in the way of practical features.

2 Choose the right plant for the right place, be it dry soil, shade, wet soil or a scorching spot, needed by sun lovers such as the day lily (*Hermerocallis*). There are plants to suit all conditions.

3 If you're buying plants for a particular bedding scheme, stand them in a group at the garden centre to see how they look together.

4 Make a list before you go to the garden centre. Then you stand a chance of coming back with what you need rather than with what catches your eye.

5 When you're planning to plant something, look at other gardens in your area first, to see if it does well in the local soil.

from The Radio Times

Features of language use in Extract B

- It uses the **imperative**: 'Don't', 'Choose', 'stand them', 'Make a list', etc.
- It uses the **second person**: the writer addresses 'you' the reader, telling you what to do.
- The words chosen are mainly simple, with a lot of monosyllabic words.
- The adjectives are chosen to make the meaning clear rather than for descriptive effect.

This is rather a different kind of writing from Extract A because it is giving you opinions. However, the opinions are based on a vast factual knowledge about plants and gardens and therefore are not what you would describe as **prejudiced** or **biased**. They are practical tips based on a lifetime's experience in gardening. For instance, Tip 2 is based on the fact that different types of plants require different conditions to grow in. The advice given is unlikely to be directly contradicted by anyone either knowledgeable or sensible, although of course other experts might not give exactly the same advice.

Activity 1.8b	Choose a piece of text that has been written to give people advice of some kind. Looking at the same aspects analysed above (language, use of first, second or third person, choice of words, etc.), make a list of points about the way the piece is written. Sum up by deciding whether it is more concerned with giving information or opinions, or whether it is a mixture of the two.

Other kinds of advice

Advice at times is much less objective than the advice given by Alan Titchmarsh. A good example of advice that is very much more opinion than fact is the kind you find in 'agony aunt' columns. Extract C opposite is an example of an answer written to a man in his forties who said he had loved another woman for twenty years, during which time she had married, brought up a family and recently got divorced. He was asking whether it was too late to let her know his feelings.

Activity 1.8c	No one would be likely to describe this reply as factual. Discuss it in your group and try to answer the following questions.
	1 Does the answer give any information?
	2 Is the reply in the first, second or third person? What is the effect of the writer's choice?
	3 What kind of tone does the writer use?
	4 What kind of adjectives does the writer choose and what effect do they have?
	5 Would you describe this reply as biased or prejudiced, or does it simply convey opinions?

Analysing a broadsheet leading article

Extract D is a leading article from *The Guardian*, which covers much of the same ground as the leading article from the *Daily Mail* in Unit 1.7 (page 43).

Extract
C

Only you can make this decision. Frankly, if you've waited twenty years to declare yourself, it may be that you don't really want a full-blown relationship. Perhaps you're happier with a fantasy love-life, where you never have to risk rejection or the messy consequence of real feelings. Sorry if this sounds blunt, but it's the question you need to ask yourself.

Extract
D

TONY BLAIR'S VISIT to the White House is one of the pivotal moments in the Iraq crisis. But this latest foreign visit is also a pivotal moment in Mr Blair's own domestic premiership too. In politics, even more than in other activities, everything is always connected to everything else. If there is a crisis in one part of the government's project, the effects of it are felt everywhere. The Iraq war has to be seen not just as a major polarising issue in its own right, but also as an episode which sends powerful ripples of doubt across the whole of the rest of the political landscape. Iraq could be a catalyst for a new, and much tougher, phase in Labour's hitherto largely unchallenged political ascendancy. It could be a lightning rod for pent-up and far less generous judgments about many aspects of the Blair project. It is one of those moments in politics that simply makes everything else look different.

This is bad news for Mr Blair, as some recent random events show. In the last couple of weeks, the government has abandoned its commitment to a more democratic House of Lords, has threatened the firefighters with the scrapping of the right to strike, has committed itself to a system of student finance that threatens future generations with heavy debts, has threatened to pull out of international treaties protecting the rights of refugees, and has announced that it is minded to allow Fylingdales to

Blair on the block

Iraq has changed government fortunes

become a central pillar of America's missile defence system. In the past, Mr Blair might have been able to persuade the public of the merits of one or even all of these controversial, even scandalous, stances. At worst, he would have persuaded most voters to allow their general confidence to overcome their scruples. But not today. Today it is all much harder pounding for him. Today everything feeds into everything else. Not all of that is fair, but then it was not fair either that Mr Blair had such an easy ride in the early years. What is clear is that he now has an immense task to capture the trust that used to fall effortlessly into his lap. If nothing else, the consequences for Mr Blair's continued wish to take Britain into the eurozone have been put at real hazard.

There have been controversial policies before and they did not do this sort of damage to Labour. What has changed? The answer, above all, seems to be Iraq – or more bluntly George Bush. The Bush administration is doing terrible damage to Mr Blair. Washington's aggressive world view, and Mr Blair's seemingly unshakeable desire to be its fellow traveller, have drained Mr Blair's political capital at an alarming rate. The polls, whether they are taken on the telephone or the internet, show clear, consistent and continuing patterns of damage. Mr Blair's personal ratings have slumped. The government's record is far less highly regarded than it was. The erosion of confidence in its economic competence, revealed in a YouGov internet poll yesterday, is particularly striking – nearly halved since the general election a mere 20 months ago. Rationally, that erosion of confidence makes little sense; the economic indicators for the British economy are far from bad, and are in many respects better than in other countries. The change of mood can only be fully explained as part of something more general. Increasingly, it seems as though the determination to back the US on Iraq is becoming to Mr Blair what the exchange rate mechanism crisis was to John Major – decisive evidence of a prime ministerial perversity which the voters will not easily forget or forgive in the difficult months that lie ahead.

from The Guardian, *1 February 2003*

Headlines

The headlines given to these two leading articles are interesting in themselves: 'Fighting a war on two fronts' and 'Blair on the block'.

It is well-known that Iain Duncan Smith describes himself as 'the quiet man', hence the satirical heading 'Invisible men'. It certainly might come as a surprise that a newspaper that supposedly supports the Conservatives should describe them as 'invisible, unheard, ineffective and irrelevant' and also 'pathetic'. Similarly the *Guardian* leader sees Blair's present course of action as disastrous.

Activity 1.8d Read Extract D carefully and remind yourself of the *Daily Mail* leader (page 43). Analyse the two headlines to discover what the language and imagery suggests. Do you find them both effective or do you find one more effective than the other?

What the text says

To discover how the broadsheet leader differs from the tabloid leader, we need to analyse it in the same way as before. The broad subject-matter of the two leaders is quite similar: they are both concerned with the effect Blair's stance on Iraq is having on his standing as a prime minister. The subject-matter differs in that the second paragraph of *The Guardian* mentions briefly a range of recent government policies that it considers to be ill-judged, whereas the *Mail* concentrates on Iraq and student funding. They both finish with a reference to the Conservative Party, the *Mail* referring to the present party and *The Guardian* referring to the former Conservative Prime Minister, John Major.

It has been noted that newspapers have well-known political viewpoints. For instance, readers of *The Daily Telegraph* and the *Daily Mail* are likely to be supporters of the Conservative Party, while readers of *The Guardian* are likely to be supporters of either the Labour Party or the Liberal Democrats.

Activity 1.8e Bearing in mind the broad political affiliations we associate with the *Mail* and *The Guardian*, do you find anything surprising in the political viewpoints expressed in these two leaders?

Criticism: constructive or destructive?

We have established that both papers seem critical of political parties they might be expected to support. However, the ways in which they refer to those two parties are very different. Looking closely at the focuses of the two articles, their choice of language and tone, we can see that they have different aims.

The difference in focus

- The *Mail's* focus is on the Conservative Party leaders as a group, whereas *The Guardian* is looking just at the effect Blair himself is having on the Labour Party and the country as a whole.
- Because the Conservatives are in opposition to the government, the *Mail* concentrates on their ineffectiveness in that role, seen here as a largely destructive role; they lack 'a killer instinct'. *The Guardian* concentrates on the damage done to the UK by the pursuit of what it sees as the wrong policies.

Different language choices

- The tabloid uses a lot of critical adjectives to describe the Tories: 'invisible, unheard, ineffective and irrelevant'. *The Guardian's* language is much more measured. Blair's 'political capital' is draining away 'at an alarming rate', the polls show 'continuing patterns of damage'.
- The *Mail* makes use of slang and colloquialisms, such as 'touchy-feely', 'top to bottom', 'great black hole'. *The Guardian* uses standard English and formal register, with many Latinate words, such as 'erosion of confidence', 'economic indicators'. The closest they get to journalese is in the use of the word *slumped*.

The difference in tone

- The *Mail's* choice of very critical language to describe the Conservatives makes the tone scathing, particularly in the use of 'Pathetic!' as a complete sentence with an exclamation mark.
- *The Guardian* leader seems to have a tone more of sorrow than of anger. Words such as 'alarming' and 'patterns of damage' suggest regret at Blair's course of action rather than outright hostility, although they are balanced by 'unshakeable' and 'perversity'. There is a sense that the writer would like to support Blair if only he would turn away from his misguided course of action.

Practice in precise analysis

You can get extra practice by analysing individual sentences. For instance if you compare the opening sentences of the two leading articles, you find the following.

- They are both quite short.
- They each consist of one main clause.
- The *Daily Mail* has more polysyllabic, Latinate words than *The Guardian*. Tony Blair is described as 'commanding' and as looking 'distinctly vulnerable'. *The Guardian* describes the visit to the White House as a 'pivotal moment'.
- Both are expressions of opinion in the form of statements.
- The *Daily Mail's* opening is more concerned with the personal position of the Prime Minister; *The Guardian* is more concerned with the importance of his actions.
- The *Daily Mail* creates impact by opening the sentence with the adverb 'suddenly' and by using the superlative 'most' before the already strongly emotive adjective 'commanding'. *The Guardian's* 'Tony Blair's visit to the White House' is, by contrast, much quieter and more simply informative

When you are completing the unit activity, try to include some precise comparison of this kind.

Serious practice

UNIT ACTIVITY 1.8   Find two leading articles on the same subject, one from a tabloid and one from a broadsheet newspaper. Write a comparison of them, looking at their content, language and tone.

 WHAT EXAMINERS ARE LOOKING FOR
Leading articles or editorials contain the papers' opinions. For higher grades, you need to be able to analyse the way opinions are presented in more complex material. Examiners are looking for an ability to 'follow argument, select material appropriate to purpose' for an A grade.

Unit 1.9
Serious journalism

The unit activity is to compare two extracts from newspapers in terms of what they say and how they say it (see page 59).

Making a start

REQUIREMENTS OF THE HIGHER TIER
If you are doing the Higher Tier, you need to be able to analyse longer and more complex pieces of writing, what is often referred to as **serious journalism**. You should use the same basic method to analyse this kind of writing, but you need to be able to respond to some of the characteristics also found in the broadsheet leading article we looked at in Unit 1.8:

- a wide vocabulary
- complex sentence structures
- more difficult ideas
- greater subtlety of tone.

We have seen that serious journalism, like tabloid journalism, contains a mixture of fact and opinion. However, it can often be easier to see where tabloid journalism is putting forward opinions rather than facts, because it does so a lot less subtly than some of the in-depth, seriously researched articles to be found in broadsheets and magazines such as *The Spectator*. One of the areas much written about in serious journalism is travel. This is a topic that offers scope for a great variety of different types of writing: factual, imaginative, promotional and descriptive.

A good example of serious journalism is the article in *The Guardian*'s G2 supplement on the world's largest pharmaceutical company. The opening paragraph is given in Extract A.

Extract **A**

It is the biggest and most powerful drug company on the planet. Its state-of-the-art glass headquarters in Surrey and vast research park in Sandwich, just north of the old Cinque port, boast of the £1bn it has put into the UK economy since 1996. Its famous blue diamond-shaped Viagra pills have made it a fortune beyond the dreams of small nation states and the butt of smutty jokes worldwide.

But Pfizer's global reach has not turned the world's third largest business into a benevolent giant, according to its critics. The vast multinational stands accused of blocking reforms to global drug pricing that would help lift impoverished countries out of disease and spur their development.

from The Guardian, *24 April 2003*

Activity 1.9a Use Extract A for practice in reading more complex text.

1 Work out what you think the passage is saying and write a paraphrase of the main points.

2 List what you regard as facts in the passage and what you regard as opinions.

3 What is your overall impression of the passage? Does it seem to be:
- a balanced , objective viewpoint?
- a biased expression of the newspaper's political viewpoint?
- a mixture of the two?

Is it, overall, as far as you can judge from this brief extract, an example of responsible journalism?

A journalist's view of Sicily

Extract B is taken from an article which appeared in *The Guardian's* Travel section. The whole section was devoted to what was described as 'A 20-page Italian special'.

Extract

B

Charlie English visits the island of Vulcano, whose future relies on the elemental forces of nature that created it

Earth, winds and fire

Somewhere near the north-eastern edge of Sicily and the very toe of Italy, the tectonic plates that make up the continents of Eurasia and Africa crash into one another, one diving downwards towards the earth's core, the other being lifted high above sea level.

This faultline is one reason why there are so many volcanoes and earthquakes in the region. In recent months, you could even say it has been hectic. Mount Etna, some 3,310m high and growing, was in a near constant state of eruption earlier this winter. In October, two streams of lava boiled out of the crater and down the mountain, setting fire to pine forests and blocking the end of the runway at Catania airport. At the beginning of December, the sunken territory of Graham Island, last seen in 1831 when it was claimed by Britain, was spotted near the surface of the sea. In September, three people were reported to have died of heart attacks when a small earthquake shook the western Aeolian islands, 30km or so off the north Sicily coast.

Volcanoes created the Aeolian islands, and two of the islands' volcanoes are still active. In the Odyssey, Homer describes the resulting rugged geography of Aeolia as an "unbroken wall of bronze, and below it the cliffs rise sheer from the sea". It is here that King Aeolus, who has been given stewardship of the winds by the gods, lives in luxury with his six sons and six daughters. After playing host to the crew for a month, he helps Odysseus on his way and gives him a bag which contains the winds. The crew think it is full of gold and, when they are in sight of home, open it, releasing the winds and blowing the ship back to Aeolia, whereupon the king declares our hero cursed by the gods and sends him packing.

In the 21st century the seven Aeolian islands still have a reputation for being windy. Our destination was Vulcano, the third largest island in the archipelago, home in Greek myth to the god of fire, Vulcan. We smelled the island before we saw it, its sulphurous gases leaking from the crater drifting over the night-time sea and into the cabin or the car ferry. It was the end of summer and the area north of Sicily was covered by a noisy electrical storm. Every few minutes, lightning would rip across the sky, offering us and the handful of other tourists on the boat a glimpse of the island's 15km length.

from The Guardian, *1 February 2003*

Hint

You may need to look up some of the answers in the library or on the Internet.

Activity 1.9b   Read Extract B carefully a few times and then answer the following questions.

1 What are tectonic plates?
2 Say briefly who Homer was and what he writes about in *The Odyssey.*
3 What can you find in the first two paragraphs that is not strictly factual?
4 In what ways would you say that the third and fourth paragraphs move away from simply giving information about Sicily?
5 Does the writer present what might be regarded as a personal view here at all?

Sentence structure

The most important aspect to consider in Extract B, apart from what is fact and what is not, is the way in which it is written.

If you look at the first sentence, you can see that it is written in quite a complex way. The subject of the sentence, 'the tectonic plates that make up the continents of Eurasia and Africa', does not occur until after quite a long opening phrase. Then comes the main verb and indirect object 'crash into one another', after which the writer goes on to describe the movement of the two tectonic plates that formed the geographical feature concerned. You have to read the sentence carefully to make sure you understand exactly what is being said. The bonus for the reader in this kind of complex sentence is that the detail enables us to get a better picture of what is being described and to understand what is being said in more depth.

The overall effect of the sentence is one of careful balance. The main subject, verb and object are in the middle of the sentence, balanced by the long opening phrase before. The rest of the sentence has another good structural feature: it gives the sense of the movement of the plates in opposite directions very effectively by the balance of first 'one' and then 'the other' along with the diverging movement 'diving' and 'being lifted'.

Activity 1.9c   Look at the rest of the sentences in Extract B. Pick out two and comment on:

a) the way they are put together
b) the effect on the reader.

Paragraphing

If you look at how the writer moves from paragraph to paragraph, you can see that here also there is a good sense of structure. The first paragraph of Extract B describes what made the faultline (although it is not called that in the paragraph). She then starts the second paragraph with 'This faultline' which makes a neat connection.

Activity 1.9d   1 Briefly describe how the writer joins:

a) the second and third paragraphs
b) the third and fourth paragraphs.

Do you think she makes a good link?

Activity 1.9d
continued

2   Although this is a largely factual account, the choice of words is still important. Look carefully at the words chosen.

   a)   How many descriptive words are used?
   b)   Is there any use of metaphor or imagery?
   c)   Are there many complex Latinate words?
   d)   Are the words mainly monosyllabic, polysyllabic, or a mixture of both?

3   Comment on the effect produced by the kinds of words chosen.

4   Bearing in mind what you have discovered by doing the activities above, try to work out what the writer's purpose was in writing the article. Do you think she has achieved it effectively?

The same subject from a different perspective

The news media took great interest in the eruption of Mount Etna in the summer of 2001. Some time later, *The Guardian* published an article by Melanie McGrath, who described her visit to Etna at the time when it was erupting – see Extract C.

You can immediately see the great difference in style and content between Extracts B and C. Those differences are determined largely by the different purposes of the two writers:

- Charlie English, in Extract B, wrote her article as a contribution to a travel feature on Italy. She wanted to give information about the volcanic island of Vulcano near Sicily as a tourist destination. Because the Aeolian Islands, of which Vulcano is one, were created by volcanoes she felt that a reference to Etna would be a useful starting point. She expands on that by giving some historical and mythological background of the type that would appeal to middle-class, well-educated readers.
- In Extract C, Melanie McGrath seeks to entertain her readers by a very personal account. She is described in the introduction to the article as 'a self-confessed volcano junkie', so presumably she felt impelled to see an event that is fairly rare and arguably very exciting.

As a result there are a number of differences between the two pieces of writing, to be found in the:

- viewpoint
- tone
- choice of language
- subject-matter.

Viewpoint

We looked at viewpoint in Unit 1.8 in terms of whether the writer uses the first, second or third person and what effect that has.

Extract B is in the third person: 'This faultline is one reason ...', whereas Extract C is in the first person: 'I travelled to Sicily ...'. Writing in the third person has the effect of making us feel that the subject-matter is being written in a detached, objective way. Writing in the first person, on the other hand, has a much more personal, subjective feel to it. The personal feel is highlighted by the words 'I did this [travel to Etna] on a whim'.

Extract

C

RAGE of the
GODS

For centuries, humankind has gazed in awe at the world's volcanoes. Even today, vulcanologists are unable to predict their fiery tantrums. But for Melanie McGrath, a self-confessed volcano junkie, the power of nature's devastating time-bombs is as life-enhancing as is their will to destroy

A year ago this summer I travelled to Sicily to watch Mount Etna erupt. I did this on a whim. Police had cordoned off the roads leading to the summit, so we drove as close as we could, up to a tree-lined parking bay a few kilometres from Sapienza, where lava from the eruption had already incinerated the ski-lift and a tourist lodge, and was rolling down to meet the road above us. It was the middle of the day and the sun was obscured by cloud, the sky a dark yellow-grey and stinking. A few spectators had gathered at the cordon. A few more stayed in their cars, all the better to make a quick getaway, if it became necessary. At one end of the bay an enterprising trader had set up a stall selling coffee, panini and the little almond biscuits typical of the region. The rumble of stomachs was lost in the louder geologic grumbling, and no one had much of an appetite. Someone joked that if fate brought the lava stream our way, there might at least be time to order a decent double espresso and leave this world on a high. There was all the usual anxious camaraderie and morbid humour you get on such occasions.

Several hundred metres above us, two vast Plinian eruption columns spewed ash over Sicily. The smoke rolled like waves and there was a slight shaking of the ground. It felt as though the world was on the move. Ash came down as black rain, making a sound like the hissing of breakwater through the pines and junipers. From time to time an unnaturally hot wind gusted down, as though fleeing the summit to safety. Ash collected on my lungs and a small pile of grit settled in my stomach. It was one of those rare moments when the internal organs lose their mystery and make themselves known, just as the volcano itself was. We were suddenly intensely aware of our mortality and of the murky fragility of human offal.

At the end of the parking bay, furthest from the coffee stall, a handful of amateur vulcanologists stood on the wrong side of the police cordon, taking notes. Beside these men, in the gathering dust, lay various Heath Robinson-style gadgets – lovingly crafted, no doubt, in potting sheds as far apart as Cardiff and Sofia, from bits of old ham radio and the like. They spoke rarely, in English, in a dozen different accents, flexing the technical jargon of their hobby. Words such as pyroclastic, Strombolian, phreatic, maar and magma drifted up to meet the eggy air. They wore insouciant expressions, as if to emphasise that the boiling tumult above them was all in a day's work for men such as they, and from time to time paid grave attention to waterproof notepads and twiddled instrument dials to prove the point.

from The Guardian, *1 February 2003*

Charlie English, on the other hand, we assume travelled to Vulcano in order to report on it as a tourist destination for the paper. Since Charlie English seeks to give information about a travel destination and Melanie English seeks to record her personal impression of a visit made in special circumstance, we can reasonably conclude that they each make the most appropriate choice of viewpoint.

The personal and the more detached viewpoints also emerge from other choices made by the writers, apart from their choice of first or third person. Two other very important factors are the tone and the language.

Activity 1.9e   Look at the words in the table, which describe tone. Are they appropriate to either or both of these extracts? Copy the table and complete it.

Tone words	Extract B	Extract C
amused		
enthusiastic		
excited		
humorous		
informative		
satirical		
serious		
unsensational		

Hints

- There may be a number of changes of tone in a piece of text. A writer does not necessarily use the same tone throughout. If you think a particular word describes the tone in one of the passages accurately, find a piece of text to illustrate it.
- You may not necessarily agree that all these tones are to be found in the two pieces, or you may find other tones not mentioned here.

Subject-matter

Although both McGrath and English write about the same area, there are major differences in their focus:

- English uses Etna as a famous focus to introduce the subject of volcanic islands before going on to focus in more detail on the island of Vulcano. McGrath is concerned only with Mount Etna.
- English mentions Etna erupting, but has no personal experience of seeing it erupt. McGrath is describing something she experienced herself. English gives a lot of background information from secondary sources.
- English has little focus on individuals, whereas McGrath observes and comments on some of the other people who have gone to Sicily to see the volcano erupt just as she has.
- McGrath describes her own physical sensations, whereas English remains detached.
- McGrath gives detailed descriptions of a range of subjects from the items sold by a stallholder to the smoke and ash. English also writes of boiling lava streaming down the mountain, but as a fact rather than something she has seen.

Serious practice

UNIT ACTIVITY 1.9   Compare Extracts B and C in terms of:

- what they have to say
- the language they use to say it.

WHAT EXAMINERS ARE LOOKING FOR
For the Higher Tier you are asked to compare a piece of text used for Foundation Tier students with a more difficult piece of text. This means having a good understanding of the texts' content and being able to show how the texts are put together. The examiners are looking for 'material fully absorbed and shaped for purpose' for an A grade.

Unit 1.10
Exam focus: 1

The unit activity is a Foundation Tier question, to compare two passages in terms of their purposes, audiences and language and how well they succeed (see page 65).

Making a start

Some perspectives on charity

Read the extracts on pages 61 and 62. Extract A is an overview of the work of the Charities Aid Foundation (CAF) and Extract B is from an article in *The Guardian* about a campaign to persuade schoolchildren to be more involved with charity work.

Hint

There will be far more facts than opinions, so concentrate on finding the opinions first and then select a few of the facts to give you a feel for the difference.

Activity 1.10a Read Extract A with particular attention to what is factual in the article and what is an expression of opinion.

Copy the table and complete it so that you separate the opinions clearly from the facts.

Opinions	Facts
CAF is a charity with a unique mission.	It became an independent, registered charity in 1974.

You may be asked to write down some of the facts from a given passage and then relate them to some other information given in the passage to show your understanding. For instance, you might be asked to write down two facts from the first three paragraphs and then go on to give two reasons why it is now easier for taxpayers to give to charity than it was years ago. After writing down two appropriate facts, you might go on to say that one of the reasons why it is now easier for UK taxpayers to give money to charity is that they can do it through a special debit card set up for the purpose.

REQUIREMENTS OF THE FOUNDATION TIER

If you are doing the Foundation Tier, in the examination you will be given several pieces of text to read and some questions to answer to show that you can:

◆ distinguish between fact and opinion
◆ compare one piece of writing with another by identifying implications and recognising inconsistencies

◆ read two pieces of media text so that you can:

– write about the choice of form, layout and presentation, and how they contribute to the effect of the pieces
– look at how presentational devices contribute to the effectiveness of the pieces
– say what effects are conveyed by the print used and by any pictures.

Activity 1.10b   Find another reason why it is now easier for UK taxpayers to give money to charity.

Comparing texts: what to look for

The aspects you need to focus on in making your comparison are:

- the purposes of the two extracts
- the audiences they are written for
- their uses of language
- how well you think they succeed.

Extract

A

CAF:
AN OVERVIEW

CAF (Charities Aid Foundation) is a charity with a unique mission: to increase the resources of all charities and non-profits wherever it operates. This has been the driving force behind all of CAF's activities since it became an independent, registered charity in 1974. Its origins, however, go back to 1924 when it began life as a department of the National Council of Social Services (now known as the National Council for Voluntary Organisations – NCVO).

Now, from its Head Office in Kent, England, and with HRH Prince Philip, Duke of Edinburgh, as its Patron, CAF employs more than 350 people worldwide. Each year, the organisation distributes more than £240 million to good causes and handles over £1 billion of funds for many thousands of charities. But despite the size and scale of its operations, CAF can only achieve its mission by bringing together donors with charities, non-profit organisations and all those with an interest in creating a healthy, invigorated society.

Working with individuals

CAF's work to help individuals give more effectively lies at the very heart of the organisation. Through the Charity Account, using the world's first debit card for tax-effective giving, tens of thousands of UK taxpayers annually contribute millions of pounds to their chosen good causes. And donors can now give whenever and from wherever they choose, through the secure online donation system, All About Giving.

Such operations are not limited to the UK: in the United States, CAF's sister organisation, CAFAmerica, provides donor advised funds for those with a particular interest in supporting non-profit activity overseas. In Bulgaria, Bulgarian CAF has been able to persuade donors in its own country to match funds raised from CAF's UK donors, to tackle urgent health problems arising from the country's economic crisis.

CAF also provides a full range of trust and legacy management services. Nearly 2,000 charitable trusts are currently managed and advised in this way – all working to the maximum benefit of charity.

from www.cafonline.org

GETTING THE
GIVING
HABIT

Schoolchildren targeted in charity and volunteering drive

Liza Ramrayka

A national awareness drive launched today to promote charitable giving and volunteering by schoolchildren aims to help charities target the 57% of pupils who say they want to do more for good causes.

The drive, called Giving Nation, is being promoted by the Giving Campaign, the government-backed initiative to raise levels of donation, which is today also unveiling a fresh brand image for the Gift Aid tax-effective giving scheme.

Giving Nation will encourage youngsters aged 11 to 16 to take a more active role in the voluntary sector. It will provide teaching resources to support the new citizenship curriculum starting in secondary schools in September.

An NOP survey for the campaign, carried out among 1,125 secondary pupils, found that 76% currently helped fundraise for charity at their school. However, 57% said they would like to do more.

Giving Nation will provide teachers with free resource packs, including materials and ideas for community involvement lessons. A new website will offer online advice on organising activities, and an annual giving event, to be called G-Week, will be launched in June next

year as a focal point for fundraising and volunteering in schools.

The Giving Campaign has sent all 6,000 secondary schools a letter and flyer introducing Giving Nation. Campaign director Amanda Delew hopes the initiative will foster the next generation of charity supporters. "Young people themselves have helped us to formulate materials to stimulate this age group into why getting involved in charity is important," Delew says. "Giving Nation provides a focus for charity in the classroom and could give a boost to fundraising appeals in schools."

Schoolchildren are already a target of several high-profile fundraising campaigns, including Comic Relief and its latest spin-off, Sport Relief, and some parents have criticised the pressure they say has

been put on their children to take part.

Delew insists that Giving Nation activities will complement, rather than compete with, existing initiatives. "We're providing a framework for charitable activities that builds on young people's enthusiasm for charity and provides them with ways of getting involved," she says.

The NOP survey found that household-name charities dominated young people's awareness of giving. Oxfam topped the list, with 53% of pupils naming the charity first, followed by the NSPCC, the RSPCA and cancer charities in general – all at around 36%. Comic Relief was named by 19%.

from The Guardian,
26 June 2002

Purpose

Before you write your answer, think about the kinds of purposes people tend to have in writing information based articles. Do not forget to start with the obvious: the major purpose must be to give information! However, information may be given for a variety of purposes.

If you look at Extract B, you will probably conclude that its purpose is not exactly the same as CAF's purpose in Extract A. The Charities Aid Foundation describe their article as 'an overview', so their purpose must be to give the readers a general view of what they do, rather than giving them an in-depth coverage of one aspect of their work. The material is available on CAF's website so it is probably there to encourage interested people to find out more about the work of CAF.

Activity 1.10c   Work out what the purpose of Extract B might be.

Audience

Remember that there is a very close connection between the audience someone writes for and their purpose in writing. We said above that CAF probably wants to give visitors to their website a general view of what their work involves. So the next question is 'Who is likely to visit CAF's website?' This might include:

- people who are already interested in charity work
- people who have heard of CAF but do not really know who they are so have decided to see whether they have a website
- people who have access to the Internet
- students who are looking for information for an essay or project.

Activity 1.10d   What sort of audience do you think Extract B was written for?

Use of language

The most important thing is to find ways in which the two passages use language differently. Try to have a list in your head before you go into the exam of a few important aspects to look for when considering language – see the checklist below.

LANGUAGE CHECKLIST

- Is the piece of writing in the first person ('I' or 'we') or in the third person ('he', 'she', 'it' or 'they')?
- Are the words long and difficult or short and simple? Or are they a mixture?
- Do the words used give a lively impression or a dull impression?
- Does the passage seem very formal or is there any use of informal or slang words?

In Extract A, for instance, when looking at whether the words are long or short, you might say that there are a lot of longer words in the passage, such as 'resources', 'independent' and 'registered'.

Activity 1.10e   1   Look at Extract A again and answer the questions in the language checklist.
2   Do the same for Extract B.

Writing your comparison

So far we have been looking at the two passages separately, and you should by now have compiled quite a lot of material on both. If you want to get up into the C grade area, you need to try to make some clear comparisons between the two texts. You might find it easier if you put your material on the two passages into two columns, like this:

CAF: An Overview	Getting the giving habit
A lot of long words.	A lot of long words.
A lot of names of organisations and initials, e.g. NCVO.	A few names and initials.
Rather formal with a lot of statistics.	More lively and action-based with words like *drive*, *stimulate* and *boost*.

Activity 1.10f   Copy the table and add any other points you can think of.

As you can see, some things may be the same in both passages, for example, both have a good many long words. You could start off your comparison by making that point and then go on to look at something that is different. Your first sentence could be something like this:

Both passages contain a lot of long words, like 'organisations' and 'invigorated' in 'CAF: An Overview' and 'volunteering' and 'initiative' in 'Getting the giving habit'.

When you go on to write the next sentence, which will show something that is different between the two passages, find a suitable word or phrase to link up the two sentences, something like 'however' or 'on the other hand'.

You might decide to write about the more energetic sounding words in Extract B. Your second sentence could be:

However, 'Getting the giving habit' has more words that give it a feeling of liveliness and action, like 'launched', 'drive' and 'stimulate'.

Activity 1.10g   Practise linking sentences. Use words or phrases from the list below to link the following sentences. Use one linking word or phrase to link sentences 1 and 2 and another to link sentences 3 and 4.

Activity 1.10g
continued

1 Both writers are concerned about how to bring clean water to the millions of people who do not have access to it at the moment.
2 Both passages contain long words such as 'irrigation', 'engineering problems' and 'serious dehydration'.
3 The second writer uses some very descriptive language, with adjectives and similes.
4 The first writer has a much more economical style with very little that is descriptive.

although
and
but
despite
however
nevertheless
on the other hand

How well do you think the passages succeed?

You should not judge the passages just by whether you found them interesting. You need to think about whether they are likely to serve the purposes you decided they were written for. You also need to think about whether they are suitable for the audience they were written for.

If you thought that Extract A was written to give general information about the charity to people who are already interested in it and have access to the Internet, you would probably feel that the long words and the initials were suitable, even if not exciting. Extract B, which was written for *Guardian* readers, rather than people with a particular interest in charities, needs to be a bit more lively to keep the readers' interest.

Serious practice

UNIT ACTIVITY 1.10 Write your full comparison of Extracts A and B in terms of:

- their purposes
- their intended audiences
- their use of language
- how well you think they succeed.

WHAT EXAMINERS ARE LOOKING FOR
This is a Foundation Tier task, comparing two passages in terms of their purposes, their audiences and the language used. You need to compare them, 'identifying implications' and 'recognising inconsistencies', to use 'appropriate terminology' and to give 'clear explanation' to get a C grade.

Unit 1.11

Exam focus: 2

The unit activity is, for Foundation Tier students, to write a commentary on one media text and, for Higher Tier students, to write a comparison of two media texts (see page 71).

Making a start

In Unit 1.10 we looked at distinguishing between fact and opinion and how to compare passages in terms of audience, purpose, language and effect when answering Foundation Tier questions. In this unit, we shall look first at how to answer the media questions at Foundation level. Then we shall look at the extra requirements for responding to the questions in the reading section for the Higher Tier.

Responding to a media text for Foundation Tier

Read Extract A, and as you do so think about the various aspects of this media text you will be asked to comment on:

- form
- layout
- presentation.

Form

When thinking about form, ask yourself:

- Is the extract from a tabloid or a broadsheet newspaper?
- If it is from a tabloid newspaper (which clearly in this case it is), what sort of things are you expecting to find?

There are a number of possible answers to the second question, for example, you might expect to find:

- an emotional approach to the subject-matter (humorous, angry, sentimental, etc.)
- the use of a lot of pictures compared to text
- a prominent headline, possibly with some wordplay
- subject-matter that has a lot of human interest.

Activity 1.11a   Bearing the above four points in mind, comment on the form of Extract A.

Layout

When thinking about layout, ask yourself:
- How are the pictures presented? Is there one central picture, or two or more? How do they relate to each other? Which is the most important? Do they have good captions?
- What is the effect of the subject-matter of the pictures?
- What is the effect of the headline?
- How much text is there?
- Is the overall layout good?

Extract
A

Official Red Nose Paper

READY STEADY DOUGH

Stars roll up for launch of Comic Relief

By
TOM WORDEN
Sun Red Nose Correspondent

Here wig go, folks! Madcap stars donned red syrups and hairy plastic noses yesterday to kick off Britain's biggest charity event – Comic Relief.

Singer Gareth Gates, model Caprice and soccer legend Gary Lineker led celebrities backing this year's appeal, themed The Big Hair Do.

Organisers want people across the country to sport wacky red hairstyles to support the campaign in the build up to Red Nose Day on March 14.

So, as the official paper of the 2003 appeal, The Sun got into the spirit by sending reporter Tom Worden to meet the celebs – with his own red afro wig.

Hairy

Comic Lenny Henry launched the event in London, wearing a curly hairpiece decorated with red noses – which have sprouted FUZZ for this year's hairy theme.

He said: "This will be the biggest and best Comic Relief ever."

Comic Relief has raised over £250million for projects in the UK and Africa. Now they want your help to top 2001's £61million total.

Red Nose Day on BBC1 will involve 300 artists including Jonathan Ross, Graham Norton, Vic and Bob and Davina McCall.

The live show will feature a French and Saunders Harry Potter spoof, a celebrity Fame Academy and all-star Driving School.

Each hairy nose costs £1 and comes with a sachet of Wella styling gel. Badges, Air fresheners and T-shirts are also available.

• **TO** get your Comic Relief fund-raising kit, call 09065 500500 or see www.rednoseday.com.

Glamour curl .. Caprice styles Lenny Henry's wig yesterday

'Ang on...isn't that Deayton in beard?

Red-iculous...Lineker, in wig, and Gates

Hair he is...Sun man Tom with Caprice

from The Sun, 8 February 2003

Pictures

You need to ask yourself how well it works to have four pictures here. They are all quite similar in that they all feature celebrities taking part in Comic Relief 2003: The Big Hair Do. The bigger picture makes the theme clear because it has a girl with a hair dryer as well as a wig and hairy red nose. The effect is very colourful and cheerful, because the people are all smiling or making funny faces. The captions are amusing because they play on words, as in 'Red-iculous'.

Activity 1.11b   Answer the other questions about the layout in Extract A.
1. What is the effect of the headline?
2. How much text is there?
3. Is the overall layout good?

Presentation

Presentation and layout overlap so do not worry if you are not quite sure whether what you are writing is to do with layout or presentation. Some of the important aspects to look at with regard to presentation are:

- the sort of font which has been used, for instance bold
- the use of the headline or any straplines or captions
- how colour is used or black and white
- the overall effect of the picture or pictures.

Headline, straplines and captions

The headline 'Reddy steady dough' is a typical *Sun* headline, large, bold and based on wordplay. It makes you think of 'Ready, Steady, Go' but substitutes 'Reddy' for 'Ready' and 'Dough' for 'Go'. Because 'Reddy' and 'Ready' sound exactly the same, but have two different meanings, and because 'Go' rhymes with 'Dough', although it means something quite different, the sound and the look of the headline are both effective. Picking up on the colour red associated with Comic Relief in 'Reddy' and on the purpose of it, to make money in 'Dough' is clever and effective.

Activity 1.11c   1. Discuss the effect of the straplines, 'The Official Red Nose Paper' and 'Stars roll up for launch of Comic Relief'.
2. Look at the captions under the pictures. Do you think any or all of these are effective? Why?

Colour

The predominant effect of the whole text is of a contrast between red and black. This is eye-catching. The red is very vivid and even more so in contrast with black as on Lenny Henry's wig. The headline and strapline are black on white and white on black. They both work well because they are different from each other. Red is particularly effective because it is associated with cheerfulness, which is of course why it is the colour chosen for Comic Relief.

Activity 1.11d   Discuss the overall effect of the pictures in Extract A.

> **QUESTIONS IN THE EXAM**
> We have looked at a lot of different aspects of a media text you might be asked to write about. Some of the questions will be quite broad, such as 'How do the choices of form, layout and presentation contribute to the effect of the Item?' Some will be based on one aspect, such as 'Choose **three** presentational devices and explain how they contribute to the effectiveness of the Item.'

Responding to media texts for Higher Tier

In this section, you will be using Extract B from this unit, 'Charities – know your place', and Extract A from Unit 1.10, 'CAF: An Overview' on page 60.

Extract **B**

Charities – know your place

The voluntary sector wants a bigger role in public service provision. But charities matter most when they operate at the margins – when they protect and provide for the groups the rest of society would rather forget, *writes* **Nick Cater**

"Does charity matter?", asks this year's Charities Aid Foundation conference. The easy answer is, of course, no, since charity is at the very best a marginal part of British economic, political and other forms of life.

In economic terms, the charity industry's £15bn a year turnover (though much less is actually from individual donations) is but a small part of the incredible prosperity capitalism has delivered, and a fraction of the amount spent by the state on public services.

In political terms, charities have a very limited remit since governments decided long ago that they were not keen on subsidising those who would criticise them. Politicians take as little notice of charities as they can get away with, preferring the company and views of those who happily subsidise political parties.

In other terms – say the health, welfare and progress of ordinary people – what is more important; charity or a fully funded national health service? Charity or decent old age pensions? Charity or the best state education? Charity or the jobs, pay packets, opportunities and falling prices that are mere by-products of the far from faultless private sector's driving greed?

Compared with what the state in all its forms provides, or the wealth that companies can create, charities are very much the third sector, and should not aspire to any other place than the margins.

But the insularity of some in the charity world brings an arrogance that sometimes seems to suggest that it alone holds all the answers, providing that a few billion pounds more are diverted away from state services.

Charities trying to do too much may well fail and probably damage most of those they claim to aid.

Taking on more from the state to help deliver public services in margin-free contracts of sweated labour will destroy the independence of charities and leave the government with power but not responsibility.

Even the charity constants – paying people less than they are worth and ignoring the need for investment – will not turn charities into masters of the marketplace, and the pursuit of non-profits will ultimately damage growth and jobs.

An old media saying has it that "news is what someone, somewhere, wants to suppress; everything else is advertising".

Likewise, some of the best things that charities do is what someone, somewhere, wants stopped, censored, buried or behind bars. Look at the roles of Shelter, Amnesty, Stonewall or Sane, organisations that deal with homelessness, human rights, gay and lesbian rights and mental health respectively.

Look at the controversy that arose over the national lottery money that has been awarded to the National Coalition of Anti-Deportation Campaigns, which works for asylum seekers, and note that the community fund has now began snooping into charity websites searching for chatroom criticism of government ministers.

Charity doesn't matter much when it is doing what everyone wants – from medical research that the government could easily fund to routine housing management best left to firms and so on – since that's the easy part.

Charity matters a lot when it helps those who many ignore, deride or defile: asylum seekers, drug abusers, paedophiles and their victims, criminals, the mentally ill and so many more that are on the margins of society.

Between a government that doesn't believe in, doesn't care about and will destroy what it doesn't understand or value, and the hard, rough edges of capitalism, there's a margin a mile wide for charity that matters.

from The Guardian, *29 October 2002*

Explaining an opinion

As for Foundation Tier, you have to distinguish between fact and opinion. But for the Higher Tier, the emphasis is on recognising opinion and explaining it, rather than just identifying what is an opinion.

Activity 1.11e   Read 'CAF: An Overview' on page 60 again. Select **two** opinions. Write them down and explain how you know they are opinions.

Following an argument

Read Extract B carefully. You will be asked a question on this sort of passage to show that you can follow an argument and that you can select the appropriate material to show that. So you might be asked 'What are the reasons the article gives why charities are very important to society despite their very small income?'

Finding the material

Jot down all the points you think are relevant to answering this question. For instance, you might write:

- *Charities concern themselves with a lot of things that governments and businesses tend to ignore, such as gay rights.*
- *Charities give publicity to important subjects that powerful organisations do not want us to know about.*

When you have found all your material, think about setting it out in an effective way. This means making sure that the points follow on logically from one another and that there are no inconsistencies – unless they were present in the original argument and you want to draw attention to them.

Think of effective ways of linking your points. One way to do this is by using a linking word or phrase such as 'however' or 'nevertheless' (see also page 65). To gain the highest grades, however, you need to write with fluency and it helps to think of more sophisticated ways of linking your points. This might be through the use of a linking word within the sentence (such as 'however' in the previous sentence), or it might be by making a link in the subject-matter from paragraph to paragraph. For example, you might pick up a word or phrase from one sentence or paragraph to use as a link into the next. A similar technique is used by Charlie English in the article 'Earth, winds and fire' on page 55, where the opening paragraph describes a faultline without using that precise word. The second paragraph then opens with 'This faultline', making a clear and neat connection between subject-matter and the word that describes it.

Activity 1.11f   Complete the answer to the question:

What are the reasons the article gives why charities are very important to society despite their very small income?'

Comparing texts at Higher Tier

You will be asked to compare two texts such as the two we have here, 'CAF: An Overview' and 'Charities – know your place'. The aspects you need to compare are:

- what they say
- how they say it.

You need to make a list of points from each piece of text. For instance, for 'CAF: An Overview' you might write:

- *CAF's main aim is to increase the funds of all charities.*
- *It can only achieve its aims if it can find ways of bringing those who are willing to give together with the charities themselves.*

Similarly in relation to the other article, you might write:

- *Charities play a very marginal part in British life.*
- *Politicians prefer to ignore charities because they can be critical.*

You can complete the lists for yourself. You then need to think about how the articles use language. You might note that the CAF article is very informative, but rather dull and written in third person. The other article is also written in the third person, but it makes use of direct speech and asks a lot of rhetorical questions. These make it a lot less dull than the CAF article.

Tone

When you are comparing pieces of text, it is important to notice any differences of tone. The tone of the CAF article is very earnest, whereas the tone of 'Charities …' is much more varied. You might use the following words to describe the tone of different parts of the article: questioning, critical, satirical, ironic.

Serious practice

UNIT ACTIVITY 1.11 Foundation Tier

1 Write your answer to the question:

How do the choices of form, presentation and layout contribute to the effect of the article entitled 'Reddy steady dough'.

Higher Tier

2 Write a comparison of 'CAF: An Overview' and 'Charities – know your place' in terms of what they say and how they say it.

WHAT EXAMINERS ARE LOOKING FOR

Higher Tier students are asked to compare two pieces of text. For an A grade, you need to be able to 'follow an argument and select material appropriate to your purpose'. Foundation Tier students are asked to write a commentary on a piece of media text in terms of form, layout and presentation. To obtain a C, you need to show a 'clear, competent attempt to engage with media concepts' and explain clearly how 'form, layout and presentation contribute to effect'.

Unit 1.12

Exam focus: 3

The unit activity is a Higher Tier question, to compare how meaning is conveyed through print and image in two media texts (see page 77).

Making a start

Extracts A and B deal with the court case in which the actors Catherine Zeta Jones and Michael Douglas put their case for feeling 'violated' by pictures secretly taken of their wedding by *Hello!* magazine. Study both extracts carefully and think about comparing the ways in which meaning is conveyed in print and image in each one.

Comparing images

When comparing images, you have to take into account the context in which they are presented. So your response to the broadsheet image (Extract B) is affected by the headline 'Courtroom drama Spotlight turns to Zeta-Jones and Douglas in £500,000 privacy claim against *Hello!*' This is used to highlight and complement the image chosen by the paper to represent their view of the case.

Activity 1.12a

1   Bearing the point above in mind, discuss the image presented in Extract B. To help you to focus and organise your answer, consider the following:

- how many people are in the picture, who they are and who is centrally focused on
- what effect is obtained through clothing and accessories
- the significance of facial expressions and body language
- the effect of the background
- the effect of colour
- the position of the picture in relation to text
- the fact that this article is printed at the top of the front page.

2   Now turn your attention to Extract A. Consider the following:

- the fact that this article takes up almost the whole front page of the paper
- the size and positioning of the headline
- the effect of the three dots that follow the headline
- the effect of the positioning of the image of Catherine Zeta-Jones in relation to the picture of Michael Douglas
- the effect of the caption next to the picture of Douglas.

Having gathered a set of responses to both extracts, in terms of image, we will now go on to look at the accompanying texts.

Extract
A

AND THE WHINGER IS...

Catherine Zeta-Jones gave an Oscar-winning performance in court yesterday in her £500,000 wedding photos battle.

For nearly an hour and a half – the length of a feature film – she whinged about the sneak pictures of her and Michael Douglas published by Hello! magazine.

The movie stunner, 33, told the High Court she felt "violated" by the unauthorised snaps.

Pregnant Catherine, who may be nominated for an Oscar today for Chicago, also described the £1million paid for the official photos by

By Thomas Whitaker

Hello's rival OK as "not that much to us".

She insisted the gripping case was about protecting privacy rather than making money.

And she denied "gingering up" her complaints to win higher damages.

Supporting Catherine as he gave evidence later, Douglas, 58, described the £500,000 they are seeking from Hello! as a "pittance" considering the stress the photos caused them.

And best supporting actor is ...

from The Sun, *15 February 2003*

73

Matt Wells
Media correspondent

Courtroom Drama

Spotlight turns to Zeta-Jones and Douglas in £500,000 privacy claim against Hello!

With only one take to convince the high court in London that her lavish wedding to Michael Douglas had been ruined by the prying eyes of a paparazzo's lens, Catherine Zeta-Jones had obviously decided to play it straight.

For an hour and 27 minutes the Welsh-born actor, who is seven months pregnant, kept her composure and declined offers from judge and counsel to take a rest from cross-examination in the couple's potentially groundbreaking privacy claim against Hello! magazine.

With her newly acquired Los Angeles twang punctured by the occasional slip into Swansea drawl, Zeta-Jones, 33, told the court of her distress and anguish that her carefully crafted plans to protect the privacy of her "special day" had fallen apart so spectacularly. Discovering that a paparazzo had foiled the couple's elaborate security measures and sneaked out "sleazy" pictures of the reception made her feel "devastated and violated". The stress, she claimed, "continues up to this day".

Her only concern was to protect the dignity of a once-in-a-lifetime experience, and not to protect the £1m exclusive picture deal the couple had signed with Hello!'s arch-rival, OK!

The couple are claiming £500,000 from Hello! magazine for breach of confidence and invasion of privacy for publishing unauthorised pictures of their wedding in

Catherine Zeta-Jones and Michael Douglas leaving the high court yesterday after giving evidence

New York in November 2000. OK! is claiming a further £1.75m in loss of revenue.

Zeta-Jones was the first to take the witness stand: wearing a black trouser suit, a diamond-encrusted pendant and diamond earrings, she carefully perched herself on the chair provided, while a few feet away her 58-year-old husband – an "enigmatic Hollywood legend", according to one magazine quoted in court – chewed lozenges and stared blankly ahead.

She has been tipped to win an Oscar for her role in Chicago – now showing less than a mile away in Leicester Square –but the only critical judgment that mattered yesterday was that of Mr Justice Lindsay, the judge hearing the case.

Under cross-examination by James Price QC, counsel for Hello! magazine, Zeta-Jones said the "cheap and tacky" unauthorised pictures made it appear as if the guests were "doused in bad disco lighting". The picture which most offended her showed the groom spoon-feeding her at the reception: it ended up in the Sun, under the heading Catherine Eater Jones.

Fixing Mr Price with a cold stare, she said: "It's offensive because I didn't think I would want the world to see that at my wedding day all I did was eat."

In her witness statement, Zeta-Jones describes how one picture made her look large: "The hard reality of the film industry is that preserving my image, particularly as a woman, is vital to my career."

Mr Price held up an approved picture that was syndicated by OK! for $800,000 (about £490,000) to People magazine in the US, which showed Zeta-Jones feeding Douglas at the reception. He demanded to know the difference between that and the unapproved picture in Hello! that showed Douglas feeding her.

Zeta-Jones said the approved image was "a much nicer photograph". The Hello! image made it appear that her husband was "shoving the fork down my throat".

Mr Price asked: "Is the distinction that you are drawing the distance of the fork from the mouth? Is that what has...

from The Guardian,
15 February 2003

The use of text: Extract A

There are a number of interesting language features in Extract A. The tabloid focuses centrally on the issue of 'acting'. The writer cleverly takes advantage of two factors:

* that a courtroom trial is commonly seen as similar in many respects to a play acted out on the stage, with a number of people playing assigned roles
* that the protagonists in the court case are in fact both actors.

This makes it possible to use the language of acting throughout the short piece, as in 'an Oscar-winning performance' and 'the length of a feature film'.

Language use and tone

The tone of the headline is critical, with the use of the slang word 'whinger', and this is backed up by the repeated use of the word in the text itself. But the tone is not simply critical; it is also quite satirical. This tone emerges from the use of the acting imagery mentioned above. The implication is that the court case is a staged and well-rehearsed performance, organised perhaps both for publicity and to gain money through the awarding of damages.

The words chosen throw doubt on Zeta-Jones's and Douglas's claim that the stress they suffered was the central factor rather than the money. The word 'insisted' suggests that the newspaper does not believe the actor's protestations about her motives and there is a satirical ring to 'the gripping case'.

The fact that Zeta-Jones 'may be nominated for an Oscar today' underlines both the satirical intention and the acting imagery with its suggestion that she is well placed to give an Oscar-winning performance. Her husband is belittled by the paper in being described as simply a 'supporting actor'.

The typical tabloidese use of 'battle' adds to the effect of exaggeration in the text. Unlike much of the hyperbole we expect from tabloid newspapers, this has the added effect here of undermining the pair by suggesting that exaggeration is the basis of this whole affair.

You may have other ideas about how the text is presented and what effect it has and you may disagree with some of the points made above. We all react in slightly different ways to text depending on our own personal context and viewpoint.

The use of text: Extract B

Length and content

The most obvious difference between the two pieces of text is, as we would expect, that the broadsheet text is much longer than the tabloid text.

Activity 1.12b
1 Bearing that fact in mind, make a list of:
  * all the points that appear in both newspapers
  * the points that appear in *The Sun* but not *The Guardian*
  * the points that appear in *The Guardian* but not *The Sun*.

2 Discuss why you think these differences appear. You will need to take into account:
  * the purposes of each newspaper in presenting these articles
  * the audiences for whom they were written.

Language use and tone

We looked at some of the language features of the article from *The Sun*.
In comparing it with the broadsheet text, you will find it helpful, as with the
content, to look at any similarities as well as differences.

Activity 1.12c   Analyse Extract B and answer the following questions.

1   Does the broadsheet article use any language that is similar to that used
    by the tabloid?
2   Are there any choices of imagery that are similar to those used by
    The Sun?
3   Does *The Guardian* use a satirical tone in writing about the trial?
    If so, is it made apparent in the same way as in *The Sun*?
4   Does *The Guardian* make use of a variety of tones? If so, what are they?
5   Are the words chosen by the broadsheet writer in any way different from
    those chosen by the tabloid? If they are, what effect is produced?
6   What difference to the reader does the greater length of the broadsheet
    article make?
7   Are there any noticeable differences in the sentence structures and
    paragraphing of the two articles? If so, what is the effect?

**WHAT EXAMINERS
ARE LOOKING FOR**
This is for Higher Tier
students: for an A grade
you need a 'clear, detailed
comparison of how meaning is
conveyed in print and image'.

Serious practice

UNIT ACTIVITY 1.12   Write your complete answer to the question:

Compare the ways in which meaning is conveyed through print and image in
the two articles on Catherine Zeta Jones and Michael Douglas.

Exam technique

How well you do in the exam depends on how effective your exam technique
is. Here are some tips to help you to give the examiner exactly what is required.

Setting out your answers

* Do not forget the simple, obvious things such as labelling your answers
  clearly. This is particularly important where you are answering questions in
  different parts. The examiner needs to see at a glance whether you are
  answering 2(a) or 2(c), for instance. It does not matter if you answer the
  questions in a different order from the one on the exam paper as long as
  you label everything clearly.

* Fill in your front cover sheet accurately, showing how many extra sheets
  you have used.

* Read the instructions very carefully a number of times to make sure you are
  doing what is asked. Candidates often seize on a particular word or phrase,
  think they know what is being asked and miss something important.

- Write carefully and legibly. It keeps the examiner in a good frame of mind. It takes a long time to read badly written scripts and it is also very difficult to take in the flow of thought if you have to read every word slowly.

- Make plans to organise your answer in advance. If you do not make a plan, you may miss out important points or remember them when you have gone past the point where they should have been included. If you add them and put asterisks, it also makes it difficult and confusing for the examiner to read. If you have to make a comparison, make two columns and set the points about the two texts or aspects side-by-side. That way it is easier to keep comparing, rather than writing a lot about one aspect and then remembering that you are supposed to be dealing with the other one as well.

- You may find it helps to write out the question in your answer book. This has two advantages:
  - It helps to fix the question in your mind.
  - It makes it easier to keep checking back to make sure you are still answering the question.

- Remember that quality is more important than quantity. Try to write your answers clearly and concisely. If you write too much, you will probably start to repeat yourself. When you are doing homework, check from time to time to see whether you have said anything twice.

Preparing for the exam

- Read as many newspapers as you can from day to day, both tabloids and broadsheets, so that you are very much aware of the ways they present their material.
- You may find it helpful to use mnemonics to remind you what to include or how to spell difficult words. Some people remember how to spell 'necessary' by saying to themselves: 'Never Eat Cress, Eat Salad Sandwiches Always', where the initial letter of each word reminds them to use one 'c' and a double 's'. If you do not find that helpful, do not use it. It is best to use the methods that suit you.
- Learn the words given in the glossary so that you understand what they mean and can use them appropriately.
- If you are not very good at spelling, make a note of the words you tend to misspell and write them in a notebook. You can learn them more easily then and refer back to your own personal dictionary when you are stuck.

Unit 2.1
What is a poem?

The unit activity is to identify the features of a poem and comment on the effects of the features (see page 83).

Island Man

*(for a Caribbean island man in London
who still wakes up to the sound of the sea)*

Morning
and island man wakes up
to the sound of blue surf
in his head
the steady breaking and wombing   5

wild seabirds
and fishermen pushing out to sea
the sun surfacing defiantly
from the east
of his small emerald island   10
he always comes back   groggily groggily

Comes back to sands
of a grey metallic soar
                              to surge of wheels
to dull North Circular roar   15

muffling muffling
his crumpled pillow waves
island man heaves himself

Another London day

Grace Nichols (Guyana)

Making a start

How do we know what a poem is?

This may seem an odd question to ask, when you have been discussing poems in school for years. However, it is not such an easy question to answer and thinking about what makes a poem a poem may help you to discuss the poems you are studying so that you understand what makes them work. The aim in this unit is to understand some of the basic aspects that define poetry.

'Island Man'

Read 'Island Man' on page 78.

Rhyme

Rhyme is a very common feature of poetry, but has never been an essential aspect of poetry. Much of the greatest English poetry is written in **blank verse**. Blank verse has a certain kind of rhythm but its lines do not rhyme.

It is important not to look for rhyme as a necessary feature of poetry. In the twentieth and twenty-first centuries, it has become less and less important in poetry. However, you do need to notice whether the poet has used rhyme – if they have, it will be for a particular purpose. For instance, in 'Island Man' there is a rhyme between 'soar' and 'roar' in lines 13 and 15.

FEATURES OF POEMS
Some of the features that you may find in a poem include:

- a rhyme scheme
- comparisons or images
- a different appearance on the page from prose (that is, the continuous sentences of a novel)
- its own special rhythm
- a different use of sentence structure from standard prose.

Activity 2.1a

1 Look at the rest of 'Island Man' to see whether there are any more rhyming words in the poem.
2 Think about the effect of the words 'soar' and 'roar' rhyming. If you have found other rhyming words what is their effect? If not, what difference does that make to the poem?

Finding comparisons and images

Almost all poems contain imagery of some kind. At times, it is very simple and descriptive, but it can involve long, complex comparisons. The island man's home is described as an 'emerald island'. That is a simple image creating a visual image in the reader's mind of the colour of the island. However, it also uses a comparison – 'emerald' is suggestive not only of colour but also of a precious stone, so in using the word the poet implies not just that the island home is a beautiful vivid colour, but also that it is very precious to the man.

Activity 2.1b

What else can you find in the way of imagery in 'Island Man'?

1 How does the poet describe the man's island home?
2 How does she describe London?
3 Does she use simple, descriptive words?
4 Does she compare?
5 Are the images mainly simple or complex?

Looking at the poem on the page

You will have noticed that poems are easily recognisable just from their physical appearance on the page. That is largely because they are composed of lines of particular lengths, unlike prose where the sentence just continues from one line to the next until it has been concluded. The breaks in prose are in the form of paragraphs not, as in poetry, in the form of verses or stanzas.

Activity 2.1c   What do you notice about the appearance of 'Island Man' on the page?

1   Are all the lines the same length?
2   Do they all start at the left-hand edge of the text? If not, why not?
3   What effect does the layout of the poem have on you as a reader?

The individual rhythm of a poem

Each poem is unique. One of the things that makes it unique is its rhythmic pattern, that is the pattern of **stressed and unstressed syllables**. For instance, in 'Island Man':

- The first line has just one word 'Morning', which is composed of one stressed syllable 'Morn' and one unstressed syllable 'ing'.
- The last line, 'Another London day' starts with an unstressed syllable 'An', and then has three groups of two syllables, one unstressed followed by one stressed.

You can always find rhythm in a poem, although it may be irregular as in 'Island Man'. If it has no fixed pattern it is called **free verse**.

Activity 2.1d   Look carefully at another line from 'Island Man'.

1   Work out the pattern of stressed and unstressed syllables in it.
2   What effect do you think it has?
3   What is the effect of the rhythm of the first and last lines mentioned above?

Complete or incomplete sentences?

Many poems do not have the same kind of complete sentence structure that you find in most novels or other kinds of prose. This becomes obvious very often from the use of punctuation, which is often quite different from what you find in prose. If you look at 'Island Man', you will see that it has no punctuation at all.

Activity 2.1e   Discuss why you think there is no punctuation in the poem.

> **Hint**
>
> There are three lines that start with capital letters as if these were the beginnings of sentences. Is this in fact the case? If not, why do you think the poet uses them? What is the effect on you as a reader of having a lack of certainty as to where sentences begin and end?

Thinking about effects

You have found a number of characteristics of a poem (not all of them by any means), but examiners also want you to think about the effect of these aspects or techniques writers use.

For instance, you might think about why the poet only uses two rhyming words in 'Island Home'. There are various possible reasons. The word 'soar' is a little odd in the sense that it suggests going beyond the limits of things, yet is actually applied to the movement of the London traffic, while the rhyming 'roar' describes the sound of the traffic. As the whole poem is about the depressing contrast between the man's old life in the Caribbean and his present life in London, the rhyme very cleverly highlights the contrast. 'Roar' contrasts with the sound of surf from the first stanza and 'soar' with the images of 'wild seabirds / and fishermen'.

This is one example of how to comment on the effects of the techniques poets use. Now you need to try to put into your own words the effects of various techniques on you as a reader.

The effect of imagery

Earlier in the unit, we identified some examples of imagery and looked in more detail at a particular example – 'emerald island'. It was fairly straightforward to analyse and consisted of the visual and metaphoric use of the word 'emerald'.

Activity 2.1f Find another image in 'Island Man', either a simple visual one or one that makes a comparison. Comment on its effect.

WHAT TO LOOK FOR IN A POEM: A CHECKLIST

- **Rhyme:** The use of rhyme is a kind of repetition, for example, 'soar'/'roar'.
- **Repetition** of other kinds. Poetry uses many different kinds of repetition. The simplest is repetition of individual words, for example, 'groggily groggily', 'muffling muffling'.
- **Pictures or images:** Some words just describe, for example, 'blue', 'emerald', 'grey'. Some words make comparisons: 'crumpled pillow waves'.

- **The shape of the poem on the page:** Does the shape give any clues about the content?
- **Is there a line or couplet set apart?** Why might that be? A.A. Milne wrote a poem in the shape of a mouse. That kind of poem is called a 'concrete' poem.
- **A rhythm or rhythmic pattern:** Which syllables are you stressing? What effect does that have? For example, 'to dull North Circular roar'.
- **Sentences:** Are they complete or fragmented? How is punctuation used?

'Bwalla the Hunter'

Now that you have had some practice in looking at the features that define 'The Island Man' as a poem, let us look at another poem, 'Bwalla the Hunter' (page 82), to see how far the same features are evident.

ABOUT THE POEM

'Bwalla the Hunter' is a poem concerned with the Aboriginal culture. As a unique poem it is obviously quite different from 'Island Man'. However, that of course does not mean that they do not share a number of features you expect to find in poetry.

The first three stanzas are given here – you can read the rest on page 106.

Bwalla the Hunter

In the hard famine time, in the long drought
Bwalla the hunter on walkabout,
Lubra and children following slow,
All proper hungry long time now.

No more kangaroo out on the plain,   5
Gone to other country where there was rain
Couldn't find emu, couldn't find seed
And the children all time cry for feed.

They saw great eagle come through the sky
To his big stick gunya in a gum near by,   10
Fine young wallaby carried in his feet:
He bring tucker for his kids to eat.

Kath Walker
(Australia – Aborigine)

Activity 2.1g Using the same headings as before, see how far 'Bwalla the Hunter' has the same features as 'Island Man'.

Copy and complete the table.

- In the left-hand column, list some of the features you expect to find in poetry.
- In the middle column, record whether you can find them in 'Bwalla the Hunter'.
- In the right-hand column, note any ways in which 'Bwalla the Hunter' is different from 'Island Man'.

Features	Are they in 'Bwalla'?	Is 'Bwalla' different from 'Island Man'?
Use of rhyme	There are rhymes all the way through the poem, such as 'plain' and 'rain'. Some of them look like rhymes but don't sound like rhymes, eg 'slow' and 'now'. Some of them are based on longer words that don't rhyme so neatly, e.g. 'drought' and 'walkabout'.	The number of rhymes makes it very different from 'Island Man'.
Comparisons or images		
How the poem looks on the page		
Rhythm		
Punctuation of sentences		

Serious practice

UNIT ACTIVITY 2.1   Read carefully 'Abra-Cadabra' below.

Identify the features of the poem, using the same headings you used for 'Island Man' and 'Bwalla the Hunter'. Make notes to show what you have found. Try to comment on the effects of some of the features you find.

WHAT EXAMINERS ARE LOOKING FOR
You are required to 'read with insight and engagement' and to understand how writers use a variety of devices to achieve their effects. This first unit begins to look at these aspects. To obtain a grade C, you need to have a good understanding and some ability to discuss the effects of writers' techniques.

Abra-Cadabra

My mother had more magic
in her thumb
than the length and breadth
of any magician

Weaving incredible stories   5
around the dark-green senna
brew
just make us slake
the ritual Sunday purgative

Knowing when to place a   10
cochineal poultice
on a fewvered forehead
knowing how to measure a
belly's symmetry
kneading the narah pains away   15

Once my baby sister stuffed
a split-pea up her nostril
my mother got a crochet needle
and gently tried to pry it out

We stood around her   20
like inquisitive gauldings

Suddenly, in surgeon's tone she
ordered
'Pass the black pepper,'
and patted a little   25
under the dozing nose

My baby sister sneezed
the rest was history.

Grace Nichols
(Guyana)

Unit 2.2

Reading for meaning

The unit activity is to write explaining what a poem is about and what its more complex meaning or meanings may be (see page 89).

Making a start

People often find it difficult to read poetry. For that reason you need plenty of practice.

We are starting here with a poem that is quite straightforward to read and find a meaning in. Remember though that finding one way of expressing the meaning does not mean you have exhausted the poem's possibilities. Other people in your class may read the poem differently and you may find further meanings in it as you reread and discuss it with others.

This unit will help you to learn what to look for in a poem in order to work out both an obvious surface meaning and a more complex meaning.

Finding a meaning: 'The Sea'

Read carefully the poem below. Think about the meaning and follow the guidelines on the left.

FINDING MEANING IN A POEM

- Read and reread the poem a number of times.
- Work out what it is saying. It may tell a story or simply put across the poet's thoughts on a subject that concerns him or her.
- If it tells a story, think how you could retell the story in your own words.
- Make sure that your outline is logical and in the same order as in the poem.
- If it is an expression of the poet's thoughts, try to put them in your own words.

The Sea

There is no escape from the sea.
Sometimes
When you're not watching
It snatches things from your
Hands.   5
Sometimes, at your feet
It washes up
The things you'd thrown away.

Or else, those cheap earrings
A little girl had once lost,   10
Bathing in the sea,
Had grieved over,
And in the end, forgotten –
After an age, the sea
Washes up again.   15

Yashodhara Mishra
(India)

Activity 2.2a   Work with a partner.

1   When you have read the poem several times, take turns to tell each other what you think 'The Sea' is saying. It is important to use your own words as far as possible, otherwise you are not really showing that you know what the poet means.

2   When you have worked out your thoughts in this way, write down your version of the poem.

Finding secondary meanings

Look carefully at the poem again. Ask yourself whether it is quite as simple as it seems from the account of its meaning we have arrived at.

How can you tell whether a poem has a deeper meaning than the surface one? There is no certain answer to this question, but there may be indications that there is more to the poem than you might at first think.

Writers, especially poets, are often saying more than one thing at a time. English words frequently have more than one meaning, so that texts are often ambiguous – that is, written in such a way that you cannot be sure which of two or more possible meanings is the right one.

What can we find in 'The Sea' that suggests Yashodhara Mishra may have intended to say something more complex than the simple account above?

- Something you might notice is that the poem is written as though we spend all our time on the edge of the sea. The poet repeats the word 'Sometimes' and later writes 'After an age …'. These are words relating to time which suggest that we are always by the edge of the sea watching and waiting for whatever the sea gives us or takes from us.

- The poem's rather dramatic opening, 'There is no escape from the sea' also suggests that we are always in contact with the sea and that in some strange way it governs our lives.

Activity 2.2b   Look for some other things the poem says that suggest it is saying something more complex than is at first obvious.

Hints

You might come up with something like this:

In the first stanza Yashodhara Mishra writes about how impossible it is to get away from the sea. If you do not keep an eye on it, it takes your things away, but sometimes it gives you back the things you tried to get rid of.

The second stanza tells of a girl who lost her earrings in the sea when she went swimming. She was very upset, but just when she had forgotten all about it they were washed up again by the sea.

Hints

Consider these points:

- The sea may be used by the poet as a **symbol**. A symbol is something that stands for more than itself, as a rose may stand for love or red for danger. Can you find anything to suggest that the poem is symbolic?

- Poets often use a story or **anecdote** to tell us something that applies more generally to our lives. Have you found any evidence that that is the case with the story of the earrings? What more general truth about life might be expressed through this story?

- Poets often use words to make something that is inanimate (i.e. that does not have an individual life as a human being has) appear to be a person. Can you find any examples of that here? If so, what do you think is their significance? This technique is called **personification**.

More complex meanings: 'Hungry Ghost'
We have looked at a poem that was quite easy to read, although it could mean something much more complex. Now read 'Hungry Ghost' below, which is not quite so straightforward. You may guess that from just looking at the title.

ABOUT THE POET

Debjani Chatterjee is an Indian writer and poet based in the UK. She said of 'Hungry Ghost':

'Here is a poem about a very ordinary experience: going shopping with my father. I sometimes use it to explore what Wordsworth termed "two consciousnesses", i.e. the movement of the narrator between their past and their present.'

Hints

◆ *Question 1*: Read the poem carefully to find out the answer. Make some brief notes to show what your answer is and then find some **evidence** from the poem to back up your ideas.

◆ *Question 2*: You need to think about whether what she describes is something that she did on one memorable occasion or whether it is something that she did often.

◆ *Question 3*: To work out whether the poet is making a general point about life, you need to think what the poet is saying apart from her description of shopping with her father. How did she feel on this kind of occasion? What has changed since the time when she was a child? What conclusion can you draw from your answers to these two questions as to what point the poet is making?

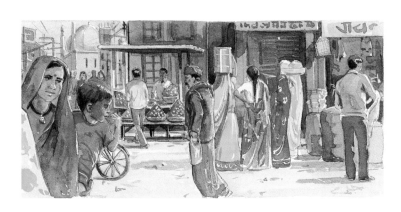

Hungry Ghost

Today I went shopping with my father
after many years. I felt I was back
in time to when I'd follow grandfather
to the market, smelling the spicy scents,
drinking the sights and mingling with the shouts.   5
Neither buyer nor seller, I would float
like a restless spirit, hungry for life.

The market is bigger. I have grown too.
There are more goods as distances have shrunk.
The prices are higher. I understand   10
about money and, alas, its bondage
of buyers and sellers. Almost I wish
I was again that hungry ghost, watchful
and floating through the world's noisy bazaar.

Debjani Chatterjee
(India)

Activity 2.2c   Follow the same method with this poem that you did with 'The Sea'. Read it several times to work out what you think the poem is about.

1   Does it tell a story?
2   Is it about a particular incident in the poet's life?
3   Is she trying to make a point about life in general or just about her own experience?

EVIDENCE

Evidence can be of two kinds:

- **a reference to what is in the poem**. You might say that the story of 'Hungry Ghost' is about a girl who used to go shopping with her father.

- **a quotation from the poem to prove your point.** If you say the poem is about a girl shopping with her father, you might then go on to quote, 'Today I went shopping with my father'.

To write a good answer in an examination you need to say what you think and prove your point with a quotation.

Other ways to find meaning

We have discovered that the poet may tell a story or reproduce his or her feelings about a particular personal experience. Some other things that will help you to find the meaning in a poem are:

- looking at the individual sentences, which may flow across a number of lines or across from one stanza to the next
- looking at the way the meaning is sometimes divided between different stanzas – the progression of points may become clearer if you can see that the flow of meaning is related to the way the stanzas relate to one another
- examining the word order, which may be different from the order of continuous sentences such as you would find in a novel
- looking up in a dictionary the meaning of any words you are not sure of.

If we look at 'Hungry Ghost' in relation to these points, we find:

- There are some long sentences but each stanza is self-contained.
- 'Almost I wish' is an example of inverted word order.
- 'Bondage' here means being restricted.

The deeper meaning

Like 'The Sea', 'Hungry Ghost' has a number of possible interpretations. Debjani Chatterjee herself says the poem is about the relationship between childhood and adult experience when she refers to 'the movement of the narrator between their past and their present'. So we would probably be right to think the poet would expect her experience to be shared by others, because she refers to another poet, Wordsworth, who also wrote about this subject.

Activity 2.2d   In a group, discuss what you think is the deeper meaning of 'Hungry Ghost'. You may come up with a number of different possible meanings.

Serious practice

Looking at a more difficult poem: 'Limbo'

'Limbo', on page 88, is rather more difficult to understand than the poems we have looked at so far. If you read a poem and find you are quite uncertain of its meaning, do not give up. T.S. Eliot, a famous twentieth-century poet, said 'Poetry can communicate before it is understood'. What he meant was that when you read poetry it has an effect on you, even though you might not feel able to explain what it is about in a precise way.

Hints

- Consider in particular:
  - what the poet says about childhood experience
  - what the poet says about the relationship of the adult to the child as she looks back
  - what the meaning of 'the world's noisy bazaar' might be.

- Always think in terms of the variety of meanings that may attach to individual words, phrases and whole poems. Remember to find evidence to back up your points.

Limbo

And limbo stick is the silence in front of me
limbo

limbo
limbo like me   5
limbo
limbo like me

long dark night is the silence in front of me
limbo
limbo like me   10

stick hit sound
and the ship like it ready

stick hit sound
and the dark still steady

limbo   15
limbo like me

long dark deck and the water surrounding me
long dark deck and the silence is over me

limbo
limbo like me   20

stick is the whip
and the dark deck is slavery

stick is the whip
and the dark deck is slavery

limbo   25
limbo like me

drum stick knock
and the darkness is over me

knees spread wide
and the water is hiding

limbo
limbo like me   30

knees spread wide
and the dark ground is under me

down
down
down   35

and the drummer is calling me

limbo
limbo like me

sun coming up
and the drummers are praising me   40

out of the dark
and the dumb gods are raising me

up
up
up   45

and the music is saving me

hot
slow
step

on the burning ground.   50

Edward Kamau Brathwaite
(West Indies)

Activity 2.2e   Read the poem individually first. Then work in groups.

1 Before you begin to discuss the poem, each write down what your reaction to the poem is and what it means to you on a first reading.

2 Then pool your ideas in the group and try to work out what you think the poem may mean. You may come up with some contradictory ideas, which is good because no poem has one simple meaning.

3 Write one viewpoint that seems to cover the whole poem, in a column on the left-hand side of a large sheet of paper.

4 Then add any other views of the poem in further columns to the right, so that you have a sheet that can show you at a glance how many views your group has.

One possible view

As a limbo stick is mentioned in the first line, I thought it must have something to do with the West Indian limbo dance, especially as these poems are about different cultures. The poet seems to be telling us readers to dance the limbo like him. The rest of the poem is quite confusing though; the poet seems to be on a ship like the slave ships of earlier times. It might be that the limbo stick reminds him of whipping slaves, 'stick is the whip'. As the night becomes day the poet says a drummer calls to him and he is saved by the music.

This would be a good start and you could put it in the left-hand column and add another view next to it. Other members of the class might have based their explanations on different meanings also suggested by the word 'limbo'.

The Concise Oxford Dictionary gives the following definitions of 'limbo':

- a West Indian dance in which the dancer bends backwards to pass under a horizontal bar which is progressively lowered toward the ground
- in some Christian beliefs, the supposed abode of the souls of unbaptised infants
- an uncertain period of awaiting a decision or resolution.

You might then work in your group to discuss how these different meanings shed light on the poem. It would be quite possible to bring them all together in a reading of the poem, which seems to work through two stories, one present, one past, coming together through the poet's voice:

West Africans now dance going under the limbo stick; in the past they went down into the bowels of a slave ship. The limbo stick is like the white man's whip … (and so on). The darkness and the water are images rather like the Christian idea of limbo and the whole experience of slavery, like a dance, requires an end or resolution.

WHAT EXAMINERS ARE LOOKING FOR
The unit activity asks you to work out any obvious surface meaning and also more complex, underlying meanings in the poem. This means 'reading with insight and engagement' in order to pick up the subtler messages the poet is giving. The more subtle your reading of the meaning of a poem, the more likely you are to obtain a high grade.

UNIT ACTIVITY 2.2   Write a short essay to explain what you think 'Limbo' means. Explain what is happening, what is being described and also what you think are the main points the poet is trying to get across to the readers. Back up your points with evidence from the poem.

Unit 2.3
The poet's concerns

The unit activity is to write an essay showing understanding of a major concern featured in two poems (see page 95).

Making a start

As we have seen in Unit 2.2, when you first read a poem you try to work out what the subject-matter is and whether there is a story. However, we found that a simple story may have a deeper meaning.

Subject-matter

There are very few poems, even simple nursery rhymes, which say nothing beyond the bare outline of a story or statement. Most are written for other purposes as well, for example to:

- explore emotional states
- develop arguments
- make social or political points.

The subject-matter of the poem is therefore like a skeleton, which the poet clothes with his or her thoughts and imagination. In using the subject-matter, the poet has a purpose, or purposes. Part of the response of the reader is to try to work out what those purposes are.

Different cultures

In this instance, the poems you are studying all have something in common: they reveal a variety of cultures from around the world and therefore also show a variety of cultural concerns. The significance of the word 'different' is that it embraces poems from *all* cultures, including the British culture. Many of the poets whose work is represented in the two clusters of poems work in the UK, but most come from cultural backgrounds outside the predominant white Anglo-Saxon culture on which British traditions are based.

Poetic purposes

Although each poet and each poem is individual, there are some common threads that connect quite diverse poems. Some of the common purposes of poets are to:

- express their personal experience
- use their own experience to explore and comment on common human experience
- entertain
- make moral points about how we behave and how we should behave
- reveal the world to us in new and imaginative ways we have not previously thought of.

Poetic purpose in 'The Sea'

Look back to 'The Sea' on page 84. We have already worked out the subject-matter and looked at what might be some deeper meanings. We can now work out why the poet wrote what she did. Of course, we cannot be sure what her purposes were, but we can make some suggestions that seem to fit with the text that we have:

- **One of the poet's purposes is almost certainly to evoke her own experience,** which probably includes having literally lost things in the sea or found treasures on the beach thrown up by the sea.

- **There is a probability that she has thought back to those experiences and realised that they are a metaphor or symbol for life itself.** Life 'snatches things' may be her way of saying that we lose things that are precious to us emotionally as well as physically.

- **She is also perhaps making a comment on how ironic life is.** We may suffer deeply because of a loss only to find later that life makes it up to us when we least expect it.

- **She is perhaps making the point that life is challenging and inescapable.** The most telling line is the opening one, 'There is no escape from the sea'. There is a chilling bluntness about the poet's reminder to us that life's challenges and its arbitrary nature affect us all.

Activity 2.3a   In your own words, write down what you think might have been the poet's reasons for writing 'The Sea'. Give evidence from the poem to back up your view.

THE MAJOR CONCERNS OF POETS FROM DIFFERENT CULTURES

We have identified that the overarching concern of these poems is the different cultures of people from around the world. Within that broad area, there are other concerns that are common either to all the poems or to a number of them.

Some of the important issues these poets write about are:

- identity
- racial and social prejudice
- alienation and homesickness
- the rituals and beliefs of different cultures

- everyday experience from the perspectives of different groups
- universal human nature, its good and bad aspects
- war and the effects of war.

As you read through your set poems, see whether they fit into any of the above categories.

Some of them may have concerns that overlap from one category to another. You may express the poet's concerns in a slightly different way from the above list.

Vultures

In the greyness
and drizzle of one despondent
dawn unstirred by harbingers
of sunbreak a vulture
perching high on broken   5
bone of a dead tree
nestled close to his
mate his smooth
bashed-in head, a pebble
on a stem rooted in   10
a dump of gross
feathers, inclined affectionately
to hers. Yesterday they picked
the eyes of a swollen
corpse in a water-logged   15
trench and ate the
things in its bowel. Full
gorged they chose their roost
keeping the hollowed remnant
in easy range of cold   20
telescopic eyes …
    Strange
indeed how love in other
ways so particular
will pick a corner   25
in that charnel-house
tidy it and coil up there, perhaps
even fall asleep – her face
turned to the wall!

… Thus the Commandant at Belsen   30
Camp going home for
the day with fumes of
human roast clinging
rebelliously to his hairy
nostrils will stop   35
at the wayside sweet-shop
and pick up a chocolate
for his tender offspring
waiting at home for Daddy's
return …   40
    Praise bounteous
providence if you will
that grants even an ogre
a tiny glow-worm
tenderness encapsulated   45
in icy caverns of a cruel
heart or else despair
for in the very germ
of that kindred love is
lodged the perpetuity   50
of evil.

Chinua Achebe
(Nigeria)

What Were They Like?

1) Did the people of Vietnam
   use lanterns of stone?

2) Did they hold ceremonies
   to reverence the opening of
   buds?   5

3) Were they inclined to quiet laughter?

4) Did they use bone and ivory,
   jade and silver, for ornament?

5) Had they an epic poem?

6) Did they distinguish between speech and singing?   10

1) Sir, their light hearts turned to stone.
   It is not remembered whether in gardens
   stone lanterns illumined pleasant ways.

2) Perhaps they gathered once to delight in blossom,
   but after the children were killed   15
   there were no more buds)

3) Sir, laughter is bitter to the burned mouth.

4) A dream ago, perhaps. Ornament is for joy.
   All the bones were charred.

5) It is not remembered. Remember,   20
   most were peasants; their life
   was in rice and bamboo.
   When peaceful clouds were reflected in the paddies
   and the water buffalo stepped surely along terraces,
   maybe fathers told their sons old tales.   25
   When bombs smashed those mirrors
   there was time only to scream.

6) There is an echo yet
   of their speech which was like a song,
   It was reported that their singing resembled   30
   the flight of moths in moonlight.
   Who can say? It is silent now.

Denise Levertov
(UK and USA)

Serious practice

The two poems on pages 92 and 93 have some common concerns.

The subject-matter of 'Vultures'

These two poems are quite complex, so you would expect to find people describing their subject-matter in a variety of different ways. For instance, you might describe the subject-matter of 'Vultures' in the two following ways:

Achebe's poem is about vultures.

'Vultures' is about the strange love vultures seem to show for one another despite the unpleasant nature of their eating habits.

Activity 2.3b   Write down briefly what you see as the subject-matter of 'What Were They Like?'. Do not think about what the poet's deeper meanings may be, but simply what she takes as the basis for expressing meaning.

The central concerns of 'Vultures' and 'What Were They Like?'

Moving away from the obvious subject-matter of the poems, we can consider what the poet's most important concerns are. Most readers would probably agree that these poems are concerned with:

* universal human nature, its good and bad aspects
* war and the effects of war
* everyday experience from the perspectives of different groups.

Universal human nature, its good and bad aspects

What evidence is there in the two poems that the poets are showing us universal truths about human nature?

* 'Vultures' shows that human beings, like vultures, are a curious mixture of good and bad characteristics. They are like the Commandant of a prison camp in Nazi Germany who presided over the genocide of the Jews but then went home to treat his own children with tenderness.
* 'What Were They Like?' shows the Vietnamese victims of war as people who lived a life of civilised traditions while the American enemy who killed their children destroyed those traditions. The poem does not specifically tell us whether the poet sees each race as capable of both sets of traits. What do you think?

War and the effects of war

It has been pointed out that some of these concerns are overlapping. For instance, in 'Vultures' the German Commandant's capacity to live simultaneously in two compartmentalised worlds is a result partly of the job he is doing as a soldier in war-time. However, you may be able to find more to say about the issue of war in this poem.

Activity 2.3c Consider the issue of war and its effects in the two poems.

1 Do you think the Commandant is meant to portray simply this one individual or does he stand for other people of a similar nature in other situations?
2 What does the poet say that suggests the Commandant's evil is vast and deep-rooted, while his tenderness is very limited?
3 What does the poet mean by 'in the very germ/ of that kindred love is/ lodged the perpetuity/ of evil'?
4 Pick out three details from 'What Were They Like' that show the violence and destruction of war.
5 More of 'What Were They Like' is devoted to the peaceful, cultured Vietnamese civilisation than to the horrors of war. Do you still get a strong feeling of the loss of the civilised way of life? If so, why do you think that is?

Everyday experience from the perspectives of different groups

- War, unfortunately, is an everyday experience in that it is always happening somewhere in the world. The two poems show the torment of war in both the East and the West.
- 'What Were They Like?' gives numerous details of the everyday life of the Vietnamese,
- 'Vultures' gives the impression that our everyday lives are a mixture of simple affection and thoughtless cruelty and repellent habits.

UNIT ACTIVITY 2.3 Using the bullet points about everyday experience given above as a starting point, write an essay about any other details of everyday experience you have found in the two poems. Provide evidence to show how you reached your conclusions.

WHAT EXAMINERS ARE LOOKING FOR
The unit activity asks you to write an essay showing understanding of a major concern featured in two given poems. You are moving from the meanings of the poems to the issues they are concerned with here. For a C grade, you need to show 'understanding of feelings, attitudes and ideas' while, for an A grade, you need to explore and show empathy 'with the writer's ideas and attitudes'.

Unit 2.4
Point of view

The unit activity is to identify and comment on two different tones in a poem
(see page 101).

Making a start

When you read a poem, one of the things you probably find yourself thinking instinctively is: Who is speaking? Think about how different studying poetry is from studying drama. You will already have studied at least one Shakespeare play, which you have probably seen either on video or in the theatre. You become aware very quickly of a number of different viewpoints, those of Romeo and Juliet or Macbeth and Lady Macbeth, for instance. What you can never be at all sure of is what Shakespeare's own view is. Poetry is rather different because it more often seems to represent a single viewpoint and we tend to assume that the voice we hear is the voice of the poet, although that is not always the case.

FINDING THE SPEAKER: A CHECKLIST

To find out who the speaker is, ask yourself:

♦ Are there any proper names in the poem which might help me to identify who the speaker is?

♦ Are there references to family relationships, 'mother', 'father', 'child', etc?

♦ Which pronouns does the poet use, for example, 'I', 'you', 'he', 'she' or 'us'?

♦ Is the poem entirely told from one person's point of view?

♦ Is what is described in the poem the poet's personal experience?

Who is speaking?

Looking back at 'Hungry Ghost' on page 86 in relation to the questions above, we discover the following things.

• There are no proper names in the poem at all.
• The poet writes about herself and her father and grandfather.
• She uses the first person pronoun 'I' throughout the poem. You may notice that, although she is writing about a recurring experience of times when she went shopping with her father, she never speaks of 'we'. Why do you think that might be?
• The poem is entirely told from the point of view of the 'I' of the poem.
• Although it is often difficult to know if what a poet writes about is their personal experience, we do in fact know that Debjani Chatterjee is talking about her own experience, because she has written about the poem and how she came to write it. She explains that it deals with her childhood memories. Bear in mind, however, that even when the poet uses the first person 'I', it is not necessarily the poet's own point of view that is being expressed.

Point of view: 'One Question From a Bullet'

One Question From a Bullet

I want to give up being a bullet
I've been a bullet too long

I want to be an innocent coin
in the hand of a child
and be squeezed through the slot   5
of a bubblegum machine

I want to give up being a bullet
I've been a bullet too long

I want to be a good luck seed
lying idle in somebody's pocket   10
or some ordinary little stone
on the way to becoming an earring
or just lying there unknown
among a crowd of other ordinary stones

I want to give up being a bullet   15
I've been a bullet too long

The question is
Can you give up being a killer?

John Agard
(Guyana)

ABOUT THE POET

John Agard comes from Guyana in the Caribbean, but moved to the UK in 1977, where he has visited many schools, talking to students about Caribbean culture to help them to understand it better.

John Agard is well-known as a performance poet. That means that he reads his own poetry for audiences, making it come alive and showing the importance of the speaking voice in reading poetry aloud.

Activity 2.4a
1 Read 'One Question From a Bullet' a few times carefully.
2 Think about the first four questions in the checklist on page 96.
3 Work out how far they apply to this poem.

ACTION POINTS
- Read
- Think
- Work out

Does the poet write from personal experience?

When is the poet not the poet?

The last of the five aspects to take into account in deciding on the poet's point of view is whether what is described in the poem appears to be the poet's personal experience.

When you think about that aspect in relation to this poem, you realise that there is a new element here. The poet writes as if he were a bullet rather than a human being. Since he cannot really be a bullet, he cannot be writing about his own experience.

That brings us to another point. Is describing personal experience the same thing as giving your own personal viewpoint? The answer is 'not necessarily'. When you describe your own experiences, something you have probably done at some point when writing your own poetry, you almost certainly do give your own viewpoint. However, you may very well express your own view of life without describing personal experience.

If John Agard is not describing personal experience here, what is he doing? Look at these four possible responses to this question:

The poet is:

* making a bullet, an inanimate object, into a human being
* imagining himself to be that human being
* expressing the kind of person he prefers to be
* wondering whether you can change the kind of person you are.

Activity 2.4b — In a group, discuss the four possibilities listed above. Do you think that any or all of them express what the poet is doing in this poem? What evidence can you find from the poem to back up your view?

The poet's purposes

Activity 2.4c — We can look at the four possibilities in more detail to work out what the poet is trying to achieve. Why do you think John Agard would choose to write from the point of view of a bullet?

Hints

♦ Think about the following points and decide whether you agree with them:
  – writing from the viewpoint of a bullet is curious and entertaining
  – the bullet represents something more than itself. It is a symbol.

♦ Bear in mind **metonymy**.

 USEFUL WORD

metonymy
A figure of speech in which a word is used as a substitute for something that is closely associated with it. An example would be speaking of 'the Crown' to mean the Royal family and the monarchy as a whole, or using the saying 'The pen is mightier than the sword' to mean that the act of writing and its effects are more powerful than warfare.

If John Agard is imagining himself to be a kind of human bullet, he is putting himself into a different mindset from the one he normally has. It may be argued that one of the major purposes of imaginative literature is to enable us to put ourselves in other people's shoes, to understand what it is to be in a completely different set of circumstances.

Activity 2.4d 1 Discuss in your group what you think is achieved by the act of imagination in the poem.
2 Work out what kind of person you think John Agard would prefer to be.

Hints

Look at the following aspects to help you:

◆ the repetition of 'I want to give up being a bullet/ I've been a bullet too long'
◆ the contrast of the bullet with other things such as 'a good luck seed'.

The final question is: Does the poet think human beings are capable of change? The answer remains uncertain, because the poem ends on a question. The poet's point of view is closely linked with the **tone** that emerges from the writing. In this case the end of the poem has a questioning tone, suggesting that the poet is uncertain about his life and his capacity to live up to his ideals.

Tone

The tone of a piece of writing can be a difficult thing to define, but it is important to work at reading tone if you want to understand more than the surface meaning.

The simplest way to approach it is to think of it in terms of **tone of voice**. You will certainly be aware of the different kinds of voices people use in speaking to you. To some extent they are related to the role of the person in relation to you. The speaker might, for instance, be your mother, your teacher, your younger brother or sister. You come to expect certain tones of voice from people according to their relationship with you.

Activity 2.4e In a group, compile a list of as many words as you can think of that describe a tone of voice. Some suggestions are given below, but you should be able to think of many more words that describe tone.

It is highly unlikely that any two people will come up with exactly the same list.

Hints

Some tone words:

affectionate	persuasive
authoritative	sarcastic
bullying	scolding
cajoling	scornful
complacent	weary
cross	wheedling

Serious practice

Activity 2.4f 1 Read the poem 'Presents from my Aunts in Pakistan' carefully a number of times.
2 In a group, discuss what you think the poem is about, its subject-matter and concerns (see Units 2.2 and 2.3).

Hints

In discussing what you think the poem is about, it might help to consider something that Moniza Alvi herself said about her own position in English society as a person who had been born in Lahore, Pakistan:

'Growing up I felt that my origins were invisible; there weren't many people to identify with in Hatfield at that time, of a mixed race, indeed from any other race, so I felt there was a bit of a blank drawn over that.'

Presents from my Aunts in Pakistan

They sent me a salwar kameez
    peacock-blue,
      and another
    glistening like an orange split open,
embossed slippers, gold and black   5
      points curling.
    Candy-striped glass bangles
      snapped, drew blood.
    Like at school, fashions changed
      in Pakistan —   10
the salwar bottoms were broad and stiff,
      then narrow.
My aunts chose an apple-green sari,
    silver-bordered
      for my teens.   15

I tried each satin-silken top —
    was alien in the sitting-room.
I could never be as lovely
      as those clothes —
    I longed   20
for denim and corduroy.
    My costume clung to me
      and I was aflame,
I couldn't rise up out of its fire,
    half-English,   25
      unlike Aunt Jamila.

I wanted my parents' camel-skin lamp —
    switching it on in my bedroom,
to consider the cruelty
      and the transformation   30
from camel to shade,
    marvel at the colours
      like stained glass.

My mother cherished her jewellery —
    Indian gold, dangling, filligree.   35
      But it was stolen from our car.
The presents were radiant in my wardrobe.
    My aunts requested cardigans
      from Marks and Spencers.

My salwar kameez   40
    didn't impress the schoolfriend
who sat on my bed, asked to see
    my weekend clothes.
But often I admired the mirror-work,
    tried to glimpse myself   45
      in the miniature
glass circles, recall the story
    how the three of us
      sailed to England.
Prickly heat had me screaming on the way.   50
    I ended up in a cot
in my English grandmother's dining-room,
    found myself alone,
      playing with a tin boat.

I pictured my birthplace   55
    from fifties' photographs.
      When I was older
there was conflict, a fractured land
    throbbing through newsprint.
Sometimes I saw Lahore —   60
    my aunts in shaded rooms,
screened from male visitors,
    sorting presents,
      wrapping them in tissue.

Or there were beggars, sweeper-girls   65
    and I was there —
      of no fixed nationality,
staring through fretwork
    at the Shalimar Gardens.

Moniza Alvi
(Pakistan)

The poet's tone of voice

Sometimes there may be one tone of voice that predominates in a poem. It may seem ironic, cheerful or sad, for instance. However, very often you can find a number of different tones of voice within one piece of writing, as in 'Presents from my Aunts in Pakistan'. We can find evidence of these tones:

- longing – the speaker seems to wish to be different and above all to fit in with the people and the society around her
- confusion – she is insecure and swings from admiration of the clothes to a preference for the English 'uniform' of denim
- admiration and appreciation – she shows awareness of the beauty of the clothes
- self-deprecation – she does not feel that she is good enough for the clothes.

Finding the evidence

In Unit 2.2 we noted there are two kinds of evidence you can give to back-up the points you make. One is the kind used above, where the tones are evidenced by reference to the content of the poem. The other kind is **textual evidence** – quotation from the poem.

Activity 2.4g

1 Find textual evidence from 'Presents from my Aunts in Pakistan' for the four tones of voice listed above. One quotation has already been found for each. Copy and complete the table by finding another suitable quotation for each tone.

Tone	Evidence
Longing	'I longed for denim and corduroy'
Confusion	'I tried each satin-silken top – was alien in the sitting-room'
Admiration and appreciation	'glistening like an orange split open'
Self-deprecation	'I could never be as lovely As those clothes –'

2 Find other examples of tone in the poem, and evidence to support it. Add these to the table.

UNIT ACTIVITY 2.4 Choose two different tones you have found in 'Presents from my Aunts in Pakistan'. Explain your choice, giving textual evidence and a short commentary, as in the example above.

AN EXAMPLE OF EVIDENCE

When you have identified the different tones in the poem and found evidence to support them, you need to be able to say *why* you chose that evidence.

Look at this example:

A tone of sadness
In the last stanza, the poet writes:

'Or there were beggars, sweeper-girls and I was there –
of no fixed nationality,
staring through fretwork
at the Shalimar Gardens.'

The poet seems to speak here with the sad, disconsolate tone of one who no longer feels she belongs. She stares 'through fretwork' at the beautiful gardens which perhaps symbolise the Indian culture. The poet is on the outside looking in, 'of no fixed nationality'.

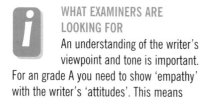

WHAT EXAMINERS ARE LOOKING FOR

An understanding of the writer's viewpoint and tone is important. For an grade A you need to show 'empathy' with the writer's 'attitudes'. This means having an excellent understanding of the writer's attitude to his or her subject-matter. For a grade C, you need to have understanding of 'feelings' and 'attitudes'. This may refer to either the writer's feelings and ideas or those of people within the poem.

Unit 2.5

Poetic structure

The unit activity is to analyse a poem to see how a variety of different techniques are used to give it structure (see page 107).

Making a start

As we have seen in Unit 2.1, one of the features we notice about poetry is that it is set out differently on the page from the prose sentences of a novel. The lines are separated from one another even where the sense of what they say carries on from one line to another.

Stanzas

Most poems have another feature in common: they divide up the lines of the poem into a number of groups called stanzas or verses. In some poems, each stanza has exactly the same number of lines as all the rest, while in others the number varies from stanza to stanza.

Looking at stanzas: 'Not My Business'

Read 'Not My Business' on page 103. Clearly this poem does have stanzas, but they are not all the same length. The first three stanzas have seven lines each, but the last one has only five lines.

Which comes first, the idea or the way of expressing the idea?

This is a very interesting question and not one to which there is an easy answer. When poets in previous generations wrote sonnets, do you think they sat down and thought 'I'll write a sonnet today' or perhaps 'I've got an idea for a poem. I'll write a sonnet' or again 'I've got an excellent idea for a poem. I think the sonnet form will suit it best'? The answer probably varies from poet to poet, but the best poems are those where the form suits the subject-matter. So we need to decide whether that is the case with 'Not My Business'.

When you ask 'Why has the poet divided the lines up in this particular way?', to answer the question you need first to work out what you think the poem is saying, because the meaning of a poem is related to its structure.

> **Activity 2.5a** Why has the poet divided the lines up in this particular way in 'Not My Business'?

Do stanzas make it easier to read the poem?

The answer to this question is 'yes', because the structure is so clear, it makes reading the poem much easier. In the same way as novelists write in sentences with punctuation to make it easier to follow the argument, the poet uses stanzas to structure his or her material. Of course an arbitrary division of a poem into stanzas would make no sense. Some poems work better with an uninterrupted **verse paragraph**. So, if there are stanzas, they should have been used for a good reason.

LOOKING AT STANZAS

As you read a poem, ask yourself:

- Does the poem have stanzas?
- If so, do they vary in length?
- Why has the poet divided the lines up in this particular way?
- How does the division into stanzas make it easier for the reader to respond to the poem?

Hints

Consider:

- the way what Osundare has to say divides neatly into four sections
- the similar structure of the first three stanzas and whether that relates to a similar content
- the different structure of the last stanza and whether that relates to a change in the content.

Not My Business

They picked Akanni up one morning
Beat him soft like clay
And stuffed him down the belly
Of a waiting jeep.
     What business of mine is it   5
      So long they don't take the yam
      From my savouring mouth?

They came one night
Booted the whole house awake
And dragged Danladi out,   10
Then off to a lengthy absence.
     What business of mine is it
      So long they don't take the yam
      From my savouring mouth?

Chinwe went to work one day   15
Only to find her job was gone:
No query, no warning, no probe –
Just one neat sack for a stainless record.
     What business of mine is it
      So long they don't take the yam   20
      From my savouring mouth?

And then one evening
As I sat down to eat my yam
A knock on the door froze my hungry hand.
The jeep was waiting on my bewildered lawn   25
Waiting, waiting in its usual silence.

Niyi Osundare
(Nigeria)

If we look more closely at 'Not My Business', we can see exactly *why* the material is ordered in the way it is. The first three stanzas tell very short stories of incidents that have occurred in the speaker's life. The first incident seems shocking, both in itself 'They … beat him soft like clay' and because the narrator is selfishly uninterested in the fate of his neighbour as long as he himself is fed and comfortable. The second stanza reinforces the same message, as does the third, making the reader feel frustrated by the indifference of the narrator. The last stanza then turns the focus around as it is revealed that it was only his own similar experience that made the poet feel for the sufferings of others.

So what we can see is that the poet chose this structure in order to reinforce the message he was trying to get across – the need for us to care about others as much as we care about ourselves.

Variations in the structure

We have noted how very similar the first three stanzas are. The last three lines of each one are identical, forming a **refrain** (something we noticed John Agard also used in 'One Question From a Bullet') which stresses the narrator's endless indifference to those around him.

ABOUT THE POET

Niyi Osundare is a Nigerian poet who came from a farming background to become a Professor at Ibadan University. His poetry is influenced by the oral traditions of his country and he often reminds his readers of the time before Africa was colonised by white men, when it had a greater sense of its own identity.

WHAT EXAMINERS ARE LOOKING FOR

Structure is quite difficult to write about. To get a C grade, you need 'awareness of authorial techniques', whereas to get an A grade you need to be able to give an 'analysis of writer's techniques'. Structure is, however, only one of many techniques used.

Activity 2.5b   In what ways does the last stanza differ from the rest? Answer these questions.

1   Why are there only five lines in the last stanza?
2   Is there any difference in the use of pronouns in the last stanza compared with the first three?
3   Is there any difference in the kind of lexis in the last stanza compared with the other three? If so, what does it suggest?
4   The yam features in the refrain of the first three stanzas. What effect is obtained by the reference to it in the final stanza?

Effects on the reader

One of the most important things you need to be able to do when answering examination questions is to say how the poet's methods affect the reader – how they produce a reaction. If you read a poem and are completely indifferent to it or do not like it, the poet has failed to achieve the effect he or she wanted. You do not have to pretend that you like all the poems you study, but if you do not like some of them, it helps if you can explain why. Just as you might explain how the poet used language or structure effectively, so you might explain why you think the writer's techniques do not work in a particular instance.

However, be warned – it is always better to try to find positive things to say about the texts you study, even if you make some less favourable comments from time to time.

Activity 2.5c   You can now use the answers to the four questions given in Activity 2.5b to work out what effects the differences in the structure of the last stanza have on the reader.

Copy the table and complete it. Some suggestions are given to get you started.

Difference in final stanza	Effect
Refrain of previous stanzas replaced by single line 'Waiting. Waiting in its usual silence'	The repeated 'waiting' and the long vowel sounds give a strong contrast to the rather jaunty refrain. Makes us realise the effect of personal experience as opposed to what happens to other people.
Use of first person in final stanza	
Narrator's emotion after indifference of previous stanzas	
Significance of yam	

Repetition

Poets use a lot of repetition. We have just noticed some examples of this:

- a number of stanzas of similar shape
- the use of a refrain
- four stories on the same theme
- individual words repeated, for example 'waiting'
- recurring objects or ideas, like the yam here.

There are other kinds of repetition that we find in poems, but these are the most obvious examples in 'Not My Business'.

Different ways of structuring a poem: 'What Were They Like?'

We have looked at the way stanzas structure a poem and at other ways of giving a poem structure through various kinds of repetition. However, each poem you read will approach the structure in an individual way.

To illustrate another poet's approach, look back to the poem 'What Were They Like?' on page 93.

Activity 2.5d Re-read the poem looking particularly at the way the poem is divided into two parts and is also given numbered sections. Why do you think the poet has divided the poem into these two parts?

Hints

Think about these questions to help you find answers:

- Which section uses question marks? Why do you think this is?
- Does the poet give any replies to the questions?
- Why is the section with the questions shorter than the other section?
- What is the reason for the numbering of both parts?

Who is speaking in the poem?

There are two speakers in the poem. One asks the questions and the other replies.

Activity 2.5e Discuss what the poem tells us or suggests to us about these speakers.

Hints

Think about:

- what you can tell from the use of questions
- any words that indicate the relationship between the two speakers
- what is indicated by the comparative length of the two people's words.

Use of repetition

Think about the ways in which repetition is used in the poem. For instance, each answer contains one or more of the significant words of the question. So the first question asks whether the Vietnamese used 'lanterns of stone'. The reply uses the word 'stone' twice in different ways. It is used in the same sense as in the question when the speaker says that their use of stone lanterns is no longer certain. It is also used in a different sense when the speaker comments that 'their light hearts turned to stone'. The effect of the repetition is therefore to highlight the destructive nature of the war in destroying the Vietnamese civilisation and numbing the people's natural feelings.

Activity 2.5f Find other examples of words in the poem which are repeated between question and answer. In each instance, say why you think the poet uses this technique.

Other uses of repetition

There are repeated pairs of words throughout the poem, such as 'bone and ivory', 'speech and singing'. They evoke the simple common things in life and give a sense of the way their life was one shared in a community.

One of the clever ways in which the poem is structured is in the last line. After the major device of a questioning opening section and an answering second section, the poet ends with a line which asks and answers a question. What do you think is the effect of this?

Structure through contrast

Structure often has to do with contrast. Here the second section is full of words that suggest doubt or uncertainty like 'perhaps' and 'It is not remembered'. The first, however, asks simple questions as though they might have simple answers. The structure suggests to us that the first speaker is very naïve and that there are no simple answers.

Different ways of structuring a poem: 'Bwalla the Hunter'

The first three stanzas of this poem were given on page 82. Now read the rest of the poem below.

Bwalla the Hunter

Big fella eagle circled slow,
Little fella eagles fed below.
'Gwa!' said Bwalla the hunter, 'he
Best fella hunter, better than me.'

He dropped his boomerang. 'Now I climb,   5
All share tucker in the hungry time.
We got younks too, we got need –
You make fire and we all have feed.'

Then up went Bwalla like a native cat,
All the blackfellows climb like that.   10
And when he look over big nest rim
Those young ones all sing out at him.

They flapped and spat, they snapped
   and clawed,
They plenty wild with him, my word,
They shrilled at tucker-thief big and brown,   15
But Bwalla took wallaby and then
Climbed down.

Kath Walker
(Australia – Aborigine)

TECHNIQUES USED TO STRUCTURE 'BWALLA THE HUNTER'

- The story
- The stanzas
- Repetition
- Rhyme
- Rhythm

The story

A story has a structure of its own, which is given by the sequence of actions it recounts. That also helps to give structure to a poem that tells a story. A story poem is a **narrative poem**. This poem illustrates the point.

The poet starts by telling us the situation, that they are hungry because of the drought, going on to give examples of the animals that have disappeared. The action comes next with the arrival of an eagle which is a successful hunter and brings a young wallaby to its young. Watching and acknowledging the creature's skill, Bwalla has an idea, climbs the tree to the eagle's nest and takes the wallaby to give food to his own family. This is a neat, simple story with a beginning, a middle and an end.

The stanzas

The stanzas give shape to the story by separating its different parts, just as chapters separate the parts of a story in a novel.

Repetition

All poems use repetition. This poem uses it in some of the same ways as other poems we have seen: the use of stanzas each with the same number of lines; the use of repeated words, such as 'Couldn't find emu, couldn't find seed'.

Rhyme

We shall be looking at this more fully later in the book, but rhyme is itself a form of repetition, the repetition of similar sounds. Sometimes the rhyming words look the same but do not sound the same.

Hints For the unit activity:

Activity 2.5g

1 Find some examples in 'Bwalla the Hunter' of the use of repetition and say how they work in structuring the poem.
2 Explain how the story is divided up between the stanzas.
3 Find examples of rhyming words in the poem.
4 Find some examples of rhyming words that look the same but do not sound the same in the poem. What difference does it make if they do not sound the same?

* Begin by thinking about:
  – what the poem means
  – the poem's concern or concerns
  – the poet's point of view.
* Then consider how Derek Walcott has used some of the techniques you discussed to structure his poem.
  – How does he use stanzas? Why are they each shorter than the last?
  – This is not a conventional story with a sequence of events. Think though about what we find instead and about how time is important in the structure of the poem
  – How does Walcott use repetition?
  – Do you notice any rhythmic feel to the poem?
  – Does the way the sentences are structured and set out seem important to you?

Rhythm

Again this is something that will be discussed in more detail later, but any rhythm has the effect of repetition. Your heartbeat gives rhythm to your body by its regular beat, speeding up at times of excitement and slowing down when you are bored. A poem is much the same. 'Bwalla the Hunter' does not have a regular rhythm in the way that older poetry tended to, but it has a strong beat. If you read it aloud the stressed syllables are very obvious, for instance 'hard', 'time', 'in' and 'drought' in the first line. In this poem, the effect of the pattern of stressed and unstressed syllables is a bit like the effect of a rap.

Serious practice

The unit activity brings together all the things you have learnt in this unit and the things you have learnt from previous units and asks you to apply them to 'Love After Love', which you may find quite difficult to understand at first.

UNIT ACTIVITY 2.5 Read 'Love After Love' carefully. What techniques does the poet use to give the poem structure?

Love After Love

The time will come
When, with elation,
You will greet yourself arriving
At your own door, in your own mirror,
And each will smile at the other's welcome,   5

And say sit here. Eat.
You will love again the stranger who was yourself.
Give wine. Give bread. Give back your heart
To itself, to the stranger who has loved you

All your life, whom you ignored   10
For another, who knows you by heart.
Take down the love-letters from the bookshelf

The photographs, the desperate notes,
Peel your own images from the mirror.
Sit. Feast on your life.   15

Derek Walcott
(St Lucia)

Unit 2.6

The language of poetry: 1

The unit activity is to write about the language choices and the effects of language in a poem (see page 113).

Making a start

Units 2.6 and 2.7 look at the different kinds of language poets use and the differing effects they create by the language choices they make. The English language is very rich in synonyms (that is words similar in meaning to one another) and there are a number of words which mean 'words' that you can use when you are talking or writing about language, including:

- diction
- lexis
- vocabulary.

What to look for in the language a poet uses

There are a number of questions you can usefully ask yourself about language when you read a poem:

- Do the words seem easy to read or difficult?
- Does the poem use a mixture of simple and complex words?
- Are there any words you do not know the meaning of?
- Do the words seem to be associated with a particular culture?
- Does the poet use dialect or standard English, slang or colloquialism?
- Does the poet write phonetically, that is in such a way as to suggest the sound of the words?
- Are there any words that seem to be closely related to one another, for example, words you associate with a particular aspect of life, such as the weather or clothing or a particular emotion such as anger or love?

When you have answered the above questions, the most important thing to do is to ask yourself how you personally react to the poet's choice of lexis.

USEFUL WORDS

slang
Very informal language, more often used in conversation than writing, such as 'bump off' instead of 'murder' or 'puke' instead of 'vomit'.

colloquialism
Non-standard use of English, such as 'He ain't coming', but often used more or less interchangeably with the word 'slang'.

standard English
The language as used by educated people with certain accepted conventions and rules.

dialect
Usually refers to regional speech, but is also used to refer to the kinds of language that make up a 'social dialect' or an 'occupational dialect', an individual use of language for a particular group.

phonetic English
English that is written in such a way as to suggest the sound of the words.

semantic field
Words used by a writer within a piece of text that relate to a common area of experience, such as war, cookery or precious gems.

syllable
All words are made up of units of sound called **syllables**. If there is only one unit of sound, the word is **monosyllabic**; if there are two or more the word is **polysyllabic**.

Looking at language: 'Presents from my Aunts in Pakistan'

Reread carefully 'Presents from my Aunts in Pakistan' on page 100.

Do the words seem easy or difficult/simple or complex?

In response to these questions most of us would probably say that the poet has used both words that are short and simple and words that are longer and more complex.

If you look at the first line of the second stanza, 'I tried each satin-silken top', you can see that the words are mostly monosyllabic and none is longer than two syllables. 'Transformation', on the other hand, from the third stanza, has four syllables, while 'nationality' in the final stanza, has five.

> **Activity 2.6a** See if you can identify the origins and meanings of some words from 'Presents from my Aunts'. How far do they match up with the information above?

Are there any words you do not know the meaning of?

Only you know which words you do not understand. The golden rule is to look up all the words you do not know and then write down both the words and their meanings and learn them.

Do the words seem to be associated with a particular culture?

> **Activity 2.6b** Find examples of any words or phrases in 'Presents from my Aunts' that you think have a connection with a particular culture. Explain what they mean and why you have chosen them.

Does the poet use dialect or standard English, slang or colloquialism?

> **Activity 2.6c** Bearing in mind the definitions given earlier, discuss whether the poem makes use of standard English, slang or colloquialisms.

Does the poet write phonetically?

The poet does not write phonetically.

Are there any words that seem to be closely related?

There are some words that form groups or **semantic fields** within the poem.

> **Activity 2.6d** Find examples of words and phrases that are closely related and list them in groups.

What effect do all these words have?

Remember that, although you have to be able to identify particular kinds of words before you can write about them, it is more important to be able to talk and write about their effect.

A WORD ABOUT ORIGINS

Over the centuries, words have come into the English language from all over the world. However, there are two major sources from which English takes its roots:

- Latin
- Anglo-Saxon.

Latin, the language of the ancient Romans, had a great effect on French, through the conquest by the Romans of the land that eventually became France. In its turn, France influenced English through the Norman Conquest, so now a lot of our words have their origins in Latin, for example, 'transformation' and 'fractured'. Some words, like 'photographs' go back to Greek origins. The shorter words such as 'shade' tend to have Old English origins.

Some questions you should ask yourself are:

- What is the effect of the poet's use of fairly formal English and a lot of long, Latinate words?
- What effect do the words relating to a particular culture have?
- What effect is achieved by using words that are related to one another by being the names of colours or by being associated with light and fire?

The effect of formal English and Latinate words, and words relating to a particular culture

You may have different views on this. Some readers may feel that the formal English with Latinate words distances them from the experience being described. They might prefer something more colloquial. However, if you think about the poet's subject-matter and purposes, you might feel that the poet uses the kind of language she does for a particular reason.

Activity 2.6e	1 Discuss your group's views on the use of formal English. Why do you think the poet uses it? Find some evidence to back up your view. Bear in mind the issue of alienation in the poem.
	2 Discuss how and why words belonging to the Pakistani culture or the British culture are used in the poem.

Words from a particular semantic field

Groups of words that relate to one another, such as the words relating to colour here, have a cumulative effect as you read the poem so that by the end you can see how they make a kind of pattern of meaning.

The words referring to the colours of the Pakistani clothes are bright and vivid ('peacock-blue', 'apple-green') or are associated with light and sheen (glistening like an orange', 'aflame'). The effect is to make the presents from abroad seem both exotic and also alien. These word groups contrast effectively with words that describe the drab ordinariness of England ('denim and corduroy', 'cardigans/ from Marks and Spencer'), articles that seem equally out of the girl's reach.

The references to gold and silver and 'mirror-work' also suggest that these clothes and jewellery are alien and do not fit in with the English culture, so the jewellery is stolen and the clothes are kept in the wardrobe and never worn outside the house.

Words are used to show both the individual and the shared

Each poet uses words in an individual way; that is what makes each poem unique. At the same time, they use words that enable groups of people to relate to them. Do not forget also that the poem we have been looking at does not just use words to show the Pakistani culture, but also words that show the English, predominantly white culture. Different groups of readers will respond to the same words in different ways, depending on their own individual situations. They might be for instance white British people, Pakistanis, British people with Pakistani origins, and so on.

Hurricane Hits England

It took a hurricane, to bring her closer
To the landscape.
Half the night she lay awake,
The howling ship of the wind,
Its gathering rage,   5
Like some dark ancestral spectre.
Fearful and reassuring.

Talk to me Huracan
Talk to me Oya
Talk to me Shango   10
And Hattie,
My sweeping, back-home cousin.

Tell me why you visit
An English coast?
What is the meaning   15
Of old tongues
Reaping havoc
In new places?

The blinding illumination,
Even as you short-   20
Circuit us
Into further darkness?

What is the meaning of trees
Falling heavy as whales
Their crusted roots   25
Their cratered graves?

O why is my heart unchained?

Tropical Oya of the Weather,
I am aligning myself to you,
I am following the movement
        of your winds,   30
I am riding the mystery of your storm.

Ah, sweet mystery,
Come to break the frozen lake in me,
Shaking the foundations of the very trees
        within me,
Come to let me know   35
That the earth is the earth is the earth.

Grace Nichols
(Guyana)

Serious practice

Jamaican English, as the language of the place where they grew up, has of course had a tremendous effect on the poetry written by Valerie Bloom and Grace Nichols. However, the apparent influence of Jamaican English may vary enormously from poem to poem, as you will see when you look closely at 'Hurricane Hits England' (page 111) and 'Tables' below.

ABOUT THE POETS

Both **Valerie Bloom** and **Grace Nichols** come from the West Indies. Grace Nichols was born and educated in Guyana in the West Indies but came to Britain in 1977. Valerie Bloom was born in Clarendon, Jamaica in 1956 and came to England in 1979.

JAMAICAN LANGUAGE

Patois
A patois is a dialect common to the people of a region or country. The English used by Jamaicans is a patois (pronounced *pat-wah*). It is standard Jamaican English or **Jamaican Creole**.

Creole
A creole is a language that results from a mixture of a European language and a local language. In this case, the European language is English and the local language is an African language originally spoken by people who were made slaves and settled in the Caribbean.

Tables

Headmaster a come, Mek has'e! Sit down
Amy! Min' yuh bruck Jane collar-bone,
Tom! Tek yuh foot off o' de desk,
Sandra Wallace, mi know yuh vex
But beg yuh get up o' Joseph head.   5
Tek de lizard off o' Sue neck, Ted!
Sue, mi dear, don' bawl so loud;
Thomas, yuh can tell me why yuh put de toad
Eena Elvira sandwich bag?
An Jim, whey yuh a do wid dat bull-frog?   10
Tek I' off mi table! Yuh mad?
Mi know yuh chair small, May, but it no dat bad
Dat yuh haffe siddung pon de floor!
Jim, don' squeeze de frog unda de door,
Put I' through the window — no, no, Les!   15
Mi know yuh hungry, but Mary yeas
Won' full yuh up, sp spit it out.
Now go wash de blood outa yuh mout'.
Hortense, tek Mary to de nurse.
Nick, tek yuh han out o' Mary purse!   20
A wonda who tell all o' yuh
Sey dat dis class-room is a zoo?
Quick! Headmaster comin' through de door
" — Two ones are two, two twos are four …"

Valerie Bloom
(Jamaica)

Activity 2.6f   The importance of 'hearing' poetry, not just seeing it on the page, has been mentioned before. When you have read the poems a few times to work out what you think they mean, try reading them aloud to each other before you decide exactly what is being said. This should help you to work out what they are about, especially 'Tables'.

Making a comparison

When you are writing about poems for the examination, it helps to be able to see the ways in which they are similar and the ways in which they are different, in other words to **compare** them.

You may find it quite difficult to find anything similar in the kinds of language used in the two poems. They are both written in English but they are very different dialects.

• You probably noted that 'Hurricane Hits England' is mostly in standard English but uses some West Indian sounding words, such as 'Huracan' for hurricane and the names 'Oya' and 'Shango' which are names of gods belonging to the Yoruba people from Nigeria. These people in previous centuries were taken from their country to become slaves in the Caribbean.

• 'Tables' uses almost exclusively the Jamaican patois. This means not only that the words themselves are different, such as 'mek' for 'make' and 'has'e' for 'haste', but that the grammar, that is the way sentences are put together, is different as well. The first sentence is 'Headmaster a come', which means 'The Headmaster is coming'.

Activity 2.6g
1 Find some other examples from 'Tables' of patois words and work out what you think they mean.
2 Find some examples of the way words are used differently in building up sentences.
3 Did you find that it was difficult to read and understand 'Tables'? If not, why do you think you were able to make out the meaning even though the poem looked so different from what you were used to at first?

What is the effect of the different kinds of language?

You need to think here of some of the things you have learnt in earlier units. One of these is the poet's **point of view**. Think about Grace Nichols' point of view in 'Hurricane Hits England'. It is an interesting poem because she uses two different points of view. Most of the poem is in the **first person**, like the poems you were looking at in Unit 2.5, but the first stanza is different. Here the poet writes using the pronouns 'it' and 'she' not 'I' and 'me'. She is using the **third person**, describing something from the outside rather than from personal experience.

Activity 2.6h
Work in a group.
1 Discuss Valerie Bloom's point of view in 'Tables'.
2 Decide what effect the different viewpoints in the two poems have.

UNIT ACTIVITY 2.6
Choose one of the two poems discussed here and write an essay about the way the poet has chosen and used particular kinds of language. Comment on their effect and say why you chose to write about that poem.

WHAT EXAMINERS ARE LOOKING FOR
For a C grade, you need to write about the writer's use of language and its effects. For an A grade, you need to examine and analyse 'specific uses of language, demonstrating their effects and effectiveness'. Writing about 'effects' is difficult and needs plenty of practice.

Unit 2.7

The unit activity is to write about a poem, exploring what the poet says about the relationship between language and identity
(see page 119).

The language of poetry: 2

Making a start

Exploring the language of identity

In Unit 2.3 we looked at some of the major concerns of the poets. One of the issues listed was **identity**. Because the poets are writing about different cultures from the mainstream British culture, they are particularly concerned about their identity.

Activity 2.7a
Discuss in groups what the word 'identity' means to you. How would you define it? What do you think contributes to your own sense of identity?

The two poems on pages 116 and 117 are very different, but are both based around the idea of the relationship between your language and your identity.

WHAT IS IDENTITY?

The Concise Oxford Dictionary defines identity as:

the fact of being who or what a person or thing is; the characteristics determining this.

To determine your own identity, you are looking for what makes you the unique person that you are. One of the factors you are likely to think of as important is your ethnic group or nationality. If you are British, you will be influenced by a number of things that are particular to the British: their geographical situation; their history; their culture; their political structures, and so on. You could, of course, belong to a particular ethnic group but be born and brought up in another country. This happened to a lot of British people whose parents lived and ruled in India up to 1947 when it became an independent nation. Similarly, a lot of people from other countries settle in Britain. This is likely to cause difficulties for the people involved, because they have to leave behind everything they are used to: places, weather conditions, types of food and clothing, sometimes family as well, and move to a land with customs and traditions that are alien to them.

'Search For My Tongue'

Read the lines from 'Search for My Tongue' on page 116 carefully a number of times. Some of the things you need to think about are:

- the different meanings the word 'tongue' has in this poem
- the effect of the poet's inclusion of some lines in her original language, Gujerati
- the inclusion not only of the lines in Gujerati, but also some lines which spell out the sounds of the Gujerati phonetically so that the reader knows how to pronounce them (This process is called **transliteration**.)
- how, if English is your first language, you might read the poem differently from someone whose first language is Gujerati
- what the point of the poem is – why might Sujata Bhatt have decided to write it?

TONGUE = A LANGUAGE

The poet's choice of title is interesting because it suggests that her tongue is something she has to 'search' for. Since most of us immediately think of a tongue as a physical part of us located in our mouths, this may at first seem rather odd. However, the close connection between the physical feature and language is also obvious because we speak with our tongue. 'Tongue' has come to have the meaning of 'language' because of this connection.

Activity 2.7b

1   Discuss the reasons why the poet includes some lines in Gujerati in the poem. What does she achieve by doing so?
2   Why does she also include the transliteration? Why is it necessary?

Hint

Think about:the importance of the sound of the words. It will help you to know that the first two lines in Gujerati are in fact a translation of the previous two lines in English. Similarly the rest of the Gujerati lines are translated in the final part of the poem.

A different focus and response from those whose first language is Gujerati

If you try to put yourself into the place of a person whose first language is different from your own, you can get an idea of how others would react differently to the poem from you. Those whose first language is not English may respond to the English words in a way similar to the way people whose first language is English respond to Gujerati. *One of the most important things about literature is that it helps us to understand how other people feel, think and live.* Sujata Bhatt helps us to do that here. If you try to speak the Gujerati lines, the difficulty you encounter would be similar to the difficulty encountered by a Gujerati speaker encountering English for the first time.

The point of the poem

*   The poet seems to be most concerned with the difficulty of dealing with two different languages, 'if you had two tongues in your mouth'.
*   She also feels that by having to use a second language, in her case English, you are in danger of losing the first. She seems to be saying that because your identity is tied up with the language you speak, the loss of your first language is equivalent to the loss of your identity.
*   However, she also writes of a 'dream' in which the tongue she has lost, seen as an amputated stump, grows back and becomes again the most important language, blossoming like a flower growing from a bud.
*   She may have written the poem not only to express her own feelings, but to give a voice to all the other people in the same predicament as herself.
*   She probably also wanted to illustrate to those of us who have not had this kind of experience, what it is like so that we are able to understand the problem others suffer.

'Unrelated Incidents'

You will have immediately spotted that the other poem printed here is rather different from the other poems in its group, although it is also concerned with language and identity. It is different in the following ways.

*   The writer is not someone who comes from outside Britain. He is Scottish.
*   His concern with language is more narrowly focused than that of the other poets. He is particularly concerned about regional accents and language variation.

From Search For My Tongue

You ask me what I mean
by saying I have lost my tongue.
I ask you, what would you do
if you had two tongues in your mouth,
and lost the first one, the mother tongue,   5
and could not really know the other,
the foreign tongue.
You could not use them both together
even if you thought that way.
And if you lived in a place you had to   10
speak a foreign tongue,
your mother tongue would rot,
rot and die in your mouth
until you had to spit it out
I thought I spit it out   15
but overnight while I dream,

મને હતું કે આખ્ખી જીભ આખ્ખી ભાષા,

(munay hutoo kay aakhee jeebh aakhee bhasha)

મેં થૂંકી નાખી છે.

(may thoonky nakhi chay)   20

પરં તુ રાત્રે સ્વપ્નામાં મારી ભાષા પાછી આવે છે.

(parantoo rattray svupnama mari bhasha pachi
aavay chay)

ફૂલની જેમ મારી ભાષા મારી જીભ

(foolnee jaim mari bhasha mari jeebh)

મોઢામાં ખીલે છે.   25

(modhama kheelay chay)

ફૂલની જેમ મારી ભાષા મારી જીભ

(fullnee jaim mari bhasha mari jeebh)

મોઢામાં પાકે છે.

(modhama pakay chay)   30

it grows back, a stump of a shoot
grows longer, grows moist, grows strong veins,
it ties the other tongue in knots,
the bud opens, the bud opens in my mouth,
it pushes the other tongue aside.   35
Everytime I think I've forgotten,
I think I've lost the mother tongue,
it blossoms out in my mouth.

Sujata Bhatt
(India)

116

From Unrelated Incidents

this is thi
six a clock
news thi
man said n
thi reason   5
a talk wia
BBC accent
iz coz yi
widny wahnt
mi ti talk   10
aboot thi
trooth wia
voice lik
wanna yoo
scruff. If   15
a toktaboot
thi trooth
lik wanna yoo
scruff yi
widny thingk   20
it wuz troo.
jist wonna yoo
scruff tokn.
thirza right
way ti spell   25
ana right way
ti tok it.this
is me tokn yir
right way a
spellin, this   30
is ma trooth
yooz doant no
thi trooth
yirsellz cawz
yi canny talk   35
right. this is
the six a clock
nyooz. belt up.

Tom Leonard
(Scotland)

**THE GREAT DEBATE:
WHEN IS LANGUAGE
'GOOD'?**

For many years there has been
an ongoing debate about the
'value' of different kinds of
language. It tended to be assumed
in the past that what we call
'standard English' was the best
kind of language and that the best
kind of pronunciation was what we
call 'received pronunciation' or RP.
RP is perhaps best characterised
as the kind of English used by BBC
news broadcasters.

It is important to remember
that language is in a constant state
of flux: it changes from year to
year, as certain words and phrases
that used to be common die out
and others take their place. This
also applies to grammar, so that
what used to be quite rigid rules
twenty or thirty years ago have now
been relaxed. Inevitably some
people would like to stick to the old
rules and that is what causes
the debate.

Activity 2.7c   When you first look at this poem on the page, you might be able to make little
sense of it.

1   Read it aloud, so that the meaning becomes much clearer.
2   Write a paraphrase of the poem, that is an account in your own words of
what the poet is saying.

A political agenda

It should be clear even from a simple paraphrase that Tom Leonard has political
points to make here through his comment on language. To draw them out and
help define your own attitude to them, consider the following questions:

• What do you think Tom Leonard is saying about the relationship between
class and language in this poem?
• What is the significance of his use of the word 'trooth' here?
• How would you feel if you switched on the television and heard the news
read as described here?
• Why do you think you answered the previous question in the way you did?

The relationship between class and language in the poem

Because this is a very controversial subject, the answers you come up with
to some of these questions will be very wide-ranging and will depend greatly
on your own background and upbringing.

Activity 2.7d   Discuss what Tom Leonard is saying about class and language.

Hints
        Think about:

    ♦ the significance of the broadcaster
being middle-class and speaking
standard English
    ♦ what Tom Leonard suggests is the
broadcaster's attitude towards the people

who listen to his broadcast – which
words show this?
    ♦ the kind of people the broadcaster
imagines his audience to be – which
words show this?
    ♦ how the broadcaster sees himself in
relation to the people who listen to him.

The significance of the word 'trooth'

You will realise that what we have been looking at here is what the poem
is saying and also what the poet's point of view is about his subject-matter.
One of the ways he makes his viewpoint clear is through his use of the word
'trooth'. He implies that the middle classes equate 'truth' with what they see as
the beauty and correctness of language. Since Leonard himself clearly disagrees
with this view, we can see that his use of the word 'trooth' is **ironic**. In other
words, he is saying one thing but meaning another, rather as you do when you
speak to someone in a sarcastic tone of voice. It seems highly unlikely that
Leonard believes in any absolute 'truth'. He suggests that the middle-class use
of language is a way of suppressing the 'truths' of other people, which may be
revealed in a great variety of ways, simply because we are all individuals.

How would you respond to hearing the news read in Scottish dialect?
This is, of course, a question that you can only answer for yourself, but if you discuss it in a group you may find an interesting variety of responses. Some of the things you might consider are:

- the difference it would make to your understanding if you came from a completely different part of the British Isles from the speaker
- whether variety and individuality in language is important
- if you think it is important does that mean that we should have broadcasters using regional dialects of the kind Tom Leonard uses
- if we did so, would that create any other problems
- whether you think that any one way of speaking English is innately superior to any other.

The reasons for your response to the idea of listening to the news as Tom Leonard presents it
Again, only you as an individual can answer this, but you will probably find it interesting to discuss with others in your group which factors might influence your response. Some of these *might* crop up in your discussion:

- your geographical location
- the kind of education you have had
- what your social background is
- the political views held by yourself or your family

Activity 2.7e   In a group, discuss your response to hearing the news read in Scottish dialect, and the reasons for your response.

Hint

Use the lists above as a guide.

The importance of the time when a poem is written
Interestingly this poem was published in 1974, nearly thirty years ago. You may have commented in your discussions already that it is very common to switch on the news today and hear newscasters with Scottish or other regional accents.

Activity 2.7f   1   Does this mean that Tom Leonard's poem is no longer relevant to us? You would not be likely to hear a newscaster using the language Leonard uses here, even if he or she had a Scottish accent.
2   Do you think we have a long way to go before we treat people equally? Or would you prefer things the way they are?
3   Consider the look of this poem on the page. Why do you think it is set out as it is and why do you think that although it has some full stops, the poem has no capital letters except for BBC?

Serious practice

UNIT ACTIVITY 2.7   Choose one of the two poems discussed in this unit. Explore what the poet says about the relationship between language and identity and comment on how successful you think the poet has been.

 WHAT EXAMINERS ARE LOOKING FOR
The unit activity relates to the assessment objective which requires you to 'read, with insight and engagement, making appropriate references to texts and sustaining interpretations of them'. The two concerns here, language and identity, are very important in both clusters of poems. A grade C requires 'understanding of feelings, attitudes and ideas' and a grade A requires exploration of and 'empathy with the writer's ideas and attitudes'.

Unit 2.8

Imagery

The unit activity is to discuss the use of imagery and its effects in a poem
(see page 125).

Making a start

In Unit 2.1, we noted that one of the things you expect to find in a poem is comparisons or images. Poets tend to look at the world with subtlety and insight, often noting the resemblances between things. For instance, in 'Island Man', Grace Nichols compares the man's pillows to waves and the island to an 'emerald'. In 'Vultures', Chinua Achebe creates an extended image of the vultures to show their similarity to human beings.

USEFUL WORDS

How should you describe these techniques when you are discussing or writing about poems? Here are some definitions:

simile
A comparison between two things that uses the word 'like' or 'as', for example, the speech of the Vietnamese is described as 'like a song' in 'What Were They Like?'.

metaphor
A comparison that does not use the word 'like' or 'as', for example, in 'Vultures', the bird's head is described as 'a pebble/ on a stem rooted in/ a dump of gross/ feathers'.

image
The comparisons of similes and metaphors are images, but poets can also use purely descriptive imagery, which does not make comparisons, for example, in 'Presents from my Aunts in Pakistan', Moniza Alvi describes her mother's jewellery as 'Indian gold, dangling, filligree'.

Activity 2.8a   Find some examples for yourself of metaphor, simile and non-comparative imagery from any of the poems you have looked at so far.

Examining metaphor

To explore metaphor in more detail, let us look again at the two poems we looked at in Unit 2.7, 'Search for My Tongue' (page 116) and 'Unrelated Incidents' (page 117).

There are a lot of different ways of using imagery. Sometimes a poet uses one main image throughout a poem and that is what Sujata Bhatt does in 'Search For My Tongue'. The title of the poem immediately tells us what the main image is, the 'tongue'.

Use the questions on the left to analyse imagery in a poem.

What is being compared with what?
What is 'the tongue', the central image in 'Search for My Tongue', compared to? This is quite a complex metaphor, so there is no single, simple answer.

ANALYSING IMAGERY

When you are analysing imagery, ask yourself:

♦ What is being compared with what?
♦ Do you think the comparison is apt and believable?
♦ How effective is it and why?

At the beginning of the poem, the poet refers to the well-known question 'Have you lost your tongue?' which is a way of asking someone why they are so silent. In this saying, the word 'tongue' stands for 'language' as we have seen in the last unit. This is an example of **metonymy**, where the part stands for the whole. 'Tongue' is part of the apparatus of speech-making but stands here for the whole process. This is a kind of metaphor.

Because the word 'tongue' equals 'language' for the poet, she speaks as if of two literal 'tongues' to refer to English and Gujerati and goes on to say that if you live in a country where you have to speak a foreign language, the 'tongue' which is your first language will 'rot and die in your mouth'. Again this is metaphorical language.

Activity 2.8b	Discuss what you think the poet means by speaking of the tongue rotting and dying? Consider:
	<ul><li>exactly what comparison is implied here</li><li>what conditions are needed for a language to 'grow'</li><li>why those conditions might not exist in the case described here.</li></ul>

Sujata Bhatt extends the metaphor comparing the tongue to an organism capable of growth or decay in the final lines of the poem. Some of the things we need to consider here to examine the metaphor fully are:

- how the poet develops the metaphor over several lines
- what the particular significance of 'ties the other tongue in knots' is; the words may remind us of some common sayings
- what the poet is enabled to do by tying one tongue in knots.

Activity 2.8c	Discuss the three bullet points above.

How effective is the image?

Whether you find an image effective is partly an instinctive reaction. The image may immediately seem apt and pleasing. If so, when you examine it in detail you will probably find out why it seemed apt. Even if the image struck you as odd, a closer analysis may convince you that it is effective.

There are a number of ways in which we might find the image of the tongue effective. The image of a flower is one of beauty, suggesting that the poet's language is also beautiful. The metaphor gives a sense of growth and vibrancy, which makes a reference to the idea of language as something constantly growing and changing. The word 'blossom' suggests flourishing, achieving the best we are capable of and is a very positive image to end the poem with. However, you might notice that all this appears to be a dream and therefore might be something the poet is not capable of achieving.

We have found a lot of metaphorical language in 'Search For My Tongue'. If you look back to 'Unrelated Incidents', you will find that language is used very differently.

Activity 2.8d   Answer the following questions about 'Unrelated Incidents':

1   Find any metaphors in this poem.
2   What images, if any, spring to mind as you read the poem?
3   Does the shape of the poem on the page have any particular significance in view of the subject-matter of the poem?

Each person will have their own answers to these questions.

Extending metaphor

Although most poets use metaphor, they do so in a great variety of ways. At one end of the spectrum, they may use individual words that are metaphorical, as Shakespeare did for instance through Hamlet's reference to 'the mind's eye'. The mind does not literally have an eye, so he is comparing the mind's capacity to imagine with the eye's capacity to see. The phrase is extremely vivid and has now become a part of our everyday language, like many other Shakespearean metaphors.

At the other end of the spectrum, the poet may use **extended metaphor**, as Sujata Bhatt does in 'Search For My Tongue', the image of the tongue being the basis of the poem and continuing throughout. In between, there are metaphors of varying length and complexity, some of which you may not notice unless you read carefully. Metaphoric language is so much a part of our normal speech that it is easy not to notice that it is actually based on comparisons as we noted in reference to 'the mind's eye'.

Lots of metaphorical expressions like 'It's raining cats and dogs' and 'She's a real gem' have been part of the English language for a long time. Many are more recent, for example, the kind of jargon which business groups use, such as having 'a level playing-field', 'singing from the same hymn sheet' or using 'blue skies thinking'.

Activity 2.8e   In a group, discuss the ways in which your normal everyday speech makes use of metaphors. Compile a list of examples.

The poem 'Half-caste' on page 123 is based on a very simple but very cleverly developed idea. It highlights the prejudice people sometimes have against people of mixed race by using a series of comparisons to show that both the natural and man-made worlds are full of beautiful and common contrasting combinations.

One of the ways in which the poet puts across the central idea of the poem metaphorically is by describing himself as 'standing on one leg'. Some of the possible interpretations of this phrase are:

*   He is one-legged, i.e. physically disabled.
*   He is like a person who tries to stand on one leg.
*   He is only half a person and therefore has to stand on one leg. This reading would suggest that there is a pun on 'caste'. In this case, it would also have the sense of 'cast' with the idea of only half-made.

half-caste

Of mixed race, for example, if your mother were white and your father black

Half-caste

Excuse me
standing on one leg,
I'm half-caste.

Explain yuself
wha yu mean   5
when yu say half-caaste
yu mean when picasso
mix red an green
is a half-caste canvas/
explain yuself   10
wha yu mean
when yu say half-caste
yu mean when light an shadow
mix in de sky
is a half-caste weather/   15
well in dat case
england weather
nearly always half-caste
in fact some of dem cloud
half-caste till dem overcast   20
ss spiteful dem don't want de sun pass
ah rass/
explain yuself
wha yu mean
when yu say half-caste   25
yu mean tchaikovsky
sit down at dah piano
an mix a black key
wid a white key
is a half-caste symphony/   30

Explain yuself
wha yu mean
ah listening to yu wid de keen
half of mih ear
ah looking at yu wid de keen   35
half of mih eye
and when I'm introduced to yu
I'm sure you'll understand
why I offer yu half-a-hand
an when I sleep at night   40
I close half-a-eye
consequently when I dream
I dream half-a-dream
an when moon begin to glow

I half-caste human being   45
cast half-a-shadow
but yu must come back tomorrow
wid de whole of yu eye
an de whole of yu ear
an de whole of yu mind   50

an I will tell yu
de other half
of my story.

John Agard
(Guyana)

123

Activity 2.8f

1   Read 'Half-caste' and discuss these possible interpretations, saying whether you think they are likely and why. Is the metaphor effective? Is it more or less effective because it can have more than one meaning? Is it possible for all these meanings to exist simultaneously?

2   The poet picks up the idea of incomplete body parts later in the poem, speaking of the 'eye' and 'ear'. He also refers to the 'mind'. How do these references help him to get across the main idea of the poem? Do they work well in relation to the idea of standing on one leg?

3   In the second and longest section, how does the poet develop the idea of aspects of life being made up of two parts?

4   Is the whole extended metaphor here effective?

These are quite difficult questions to answer. When you have tried to answer them, your teacher will be able to give you a response to compare your own with, which may give you further ideas.

Looking at the whole poem

You have been concentrating on looking at the way the poet uses imagery in 'Half-caste' but of course you will have noticed a lot of other techniques the poet uses that we have discussed in previous units, for example:

- the structure of the poem
- the writer's tone and point of view
- the kind of language he uses.

The effect the poem has on the reader is the effect of the sum total of all these aspects working together.

As you look at more aspects of a poem, try to bring them all together in your discussion and comment.

Hints

Using the initial points in the table, your paragraph might read something like this:

In writing about a half-caste's experience of racial prejudice, John Agard uses the first person, although we cannot be sure whether he is expressing personal experience or imagining how someone else might have felt. He makes his presentation vivid and immediate by using two speakers, the 'half-caste' and someone who asks him what he means by the term. The effect of the poem depends greatly on the ironic tone the poet uses, as when he speaks of 'I half-caste human being/ cast half-a-shadow'. The tone here may also be interpreted as bitter since he implies that he is regarded as only half human, therefore casting only half a shadow. The idea is highlighted by the punning reference to 'caste' and 'cast'.

Activity 2.8g

1   Look again at 'Half-Caste' and try to bring the structure, tone, point of view and language together. Copy the table and use it to set out some of your thoughts.

Structure	Tone	Viewpoint	Language
1 The poem is divided up into four sections or verse paragraphs of uneven length.	The tone is ironic throughout. This is shown by the ridiculous idea that you can use half an ear or cast half a shadow.	The poet may or may not be speaking for himself. He may be imagining what it would be like to be a person of mixed race.	The language is African-Caribbean patois. As shown by words such as 'yu', 'yuself' and 'wid'.
2			
3			

2   When you have a number of points in each column (though not necessarily the same number in each), write a paragraph that brings more than one aspect together.

Use of similes

We have seen that similes, like metaphors, are comparisons. They are only different in making the comparison more obvious by using the word 'like' or 'as'. To see how metaphor and simile work in the same poem, look back to 'What Were They Like?' on page 93.

Activity 2.8h

1   Pick out some examples of both metaphors and similes in 'What Were They Like?', noting whether the poet makes much use of either.
Copy and complete the table.

Metaphors	Similes
1 'their light hearts turned to stone'	1 'their speech which was like a song'

2   Discuss why you think the poet uses metaphors and similes in the way she does.

You probably noticed that there are very few similes and not many metaphors in the poem. The poem is effective largely because of its simplicity. For instance, the reference to 'no more buds' is very moving because it highlights the tragic deaths of young children. The language is mostly simple and peaceful, but with some very effective contrast.

We noted earlier the great difference in the use of language between 'Unrelated Incidents' and 'Search for My Tongue'. Where Sujata Bhatt uses an extended metaphor throughout her poem, Tom Leonard does not really use metaphor at all. Both of these texts are incomplete – they are taken from longer poems and you would have to read the complete poems to be certain of the full significance of the language they use. However, poems that do not use metaphor are usually written in that way for very good reasons. Two points that might be made about the extract from 'Unrelated Incidents' on page 117 are:

*   The poet does not use metaphor because he is attempting to recreate the sense of watching and listening to a news broadcast. He achieves this through the look of the poem on the page and also through the lack of metaphor. Newscasters make very little use of metaphor.
*   Like other poems that do not use metaphor, Tom Leonard's poem may perhaps be in itself a kind of metaphor, a poem standing for the poet's whole view on language use and what he sees as false perceptions of language.

Serious practice

UNIT ACTIVITY 2.8   Choose one of the poems you have studied so far to explore the poet's use of imagery. Discuss a few examples in detail, showing what comparison is being made, if there is one, and how effective the images are in the poem as a whole.

 WHAT EXAMINERS ARE LOOKING FOR
One of the most important aspects of poetic technique you need to be able to discuss is the use of various kinds of imagery. It is one of the 'specific methods of presentation' that A-grade answers need to deal with, 'demonstrating its effects and effectiveness'.

Unit 2.9
The sound of poetry

The unit activity is to write about the way a poet uses a variety of techniques to get across a message (see page 131).

Making a start

It has already been noted that it is very important to hear poetry read aloud. Take every opportunity you can to read it aloud yourself, to listen to others reading it aloud or to read a poem with two or more people delivering different lines.

Sounds in 'Blessing'

Blessing

The skin cracks like a pod
There never is enough water.

Imagine the drip of it,
the small splash, echo
in a tin mug   5
the voice of a kindly god.

Sometimes, the sudden rush
of fortune. The municipal pipe bursts,
silver crashes to the ground
and the flow has found   10
a roar of tongues. From the huts,
a congregation: every man and woman
child for streets around
butts in, with pots,
brass, copper, aluminium,   15
plastic buckets,
frantic hands,

and naked children
screaming in the liquid sun,
their highlights polished to perfection,   20
flashing light,
as the blessing sings
over their small bones.

Imtiaz Dharker
(India)

Activity 2.9a   Read 'Blessing' on page 126.

1   Find examples of alliteration, assonance, sibilance and onomatopoeia in the poem.
2   Write about the effect each example has on the reader.

Copy and complete the tables. Some examples are given to help you.

Examples of alliteration	The effect they have
1 'and the flow has found a roar of tongues.'	1 The poem is about drought and the importance water assumes because of its lack. So when water becomes available, it is ecstatically welcomed by the whole population. The alliteration of the letter 'f' in 'flow' and 'found' helps to evoke this feeling. 'Flow' is a soft word, because of the 'f' sound and the long vowel, suggestive of the liquid nature of water and its movement. The repeated 'f' in 'found' connects the nature of the water with the human benefit it confers. It makes everyone shout with joy. It also suggests something 'found', the 'Blessing' of the title.
2 'their highlights polished to perfection …'	
3	

Examples of assonance	The effect they have
1 'Imagine the drip of it, the small splash, echo in a tin mug'	1 These three lines contain three examples of a short 'i' sound in 'drip', 'it' and 'tin'. They also pick up on similar sounds in the first two lines of the poem, 'skin' and 'is'. The short sound, each time in a monosyllabic word, reinforces the scarcity of the water, which only comes in 'drips'.
2	
3	

Examples of sibilance	The effect they have
1 'as the blessing sings over their small bones.'	1 The example contains five words with 's' sounds distributed throughout the lines. Sibilance often runs through a line or several lines. These two lines form the conclusion to the poem and are a celebration of water, which is the basis of life. The repeated 's' sound here gives a whispering vitality to the lines, suggesting both the movement and sound of water itself and the sound of joy in the people's singing as they celebrate the water. The whispering, rustling sound of the letter 's' is sometimes called a 'sussuration', itself another sibilant word.
2	
3	

Examples of onomatopeia	The effect they have
1 'The municipal pipe bursts,'	1 The word 'bursts' is suggestive of the sound and movement involved: a sudden explosion of noise.

Hints

You will find that there is some overlap. For instance, the lines of repeated short 'i' sounds also use onomatopoeia. The word 'drip' echoes the sense, as does 'splash'. You might be able to find an example from a poem which illustrates all four techniques simultaneously.

USEFUL WORDS

alliteration
The repetition of a consonant in a line or lines of poetry, usually at the beginnings of words, as in 'the soft labouring of my lungs' where the 'l' is repeated in 'Nothing's Changed' by Tatamkhulu Afrika (page 128).

assonance
The repetition of a vowel sound in a line or lines of poetry, as in the repeated 'u' sound in: 'muffling muffling/ his crumpled pillow waves' in 'Island Man' by Grace Nichols.

sibilance
Repeated 's' sounds in poetry as in the opening lines of 'The Vultures' by Chinua Achebe:

'In the greyness
and drizzle of one despondent
dawn unstirred by harbingers
of sunbreak …'

Notice here that the 's' sounds do not necessarily come at the beginnings of words and that the 'z' sound adds to the effect.

onomatopoeia
A technique of choosing a word which has a sound that echoes its meaning, such as 'splash', 'crash', 'drip'. A good example can be found in 'Blessing' by Imtiaz Dharker.

Nothing's Changed

Small round hard stones click
under my heels,
seeding grasses thrust
bearded seeds
into trouser cuffs, cans,   5
trodden on, crunch
in tall, purple-flowering,
amiable weeds.

District Six.
No board says it is: 10
but my feet know;
and my hands,
and the skin about my bones,
and the soft labouring of my lungs,
and the hot, white, inwards turning   15
anger of my eyes.

Brash with grass.
name flaring like a flag,
it squats
in the grass and weeds,   20
incipient Port Jackson trees;
new, up-market, haute cuisine,
guard at the gatepost,
whites only inn.

No sign says it is: 25
but we know where we belong.

I press my nose
to the clear panes, know,
before I see them, there will be
crushed ice white glass,   30
linen falls,
the single rose.

Down the road,
working man's café sells
bunny chows.   35
Take it with you, eat
it at a plastic table's top,
wipe your fingers on your jeans,
spit a little on the floor:
it's in the bone.   40

I back from the glass,
boy again,
leaving small mean O
of small, mean mouth.
Hands burn   45
for a stone, a bomb,
to shiver down the glass.
Nothing's changed.

Tatamkhulu Afrika
(South Africa)

ABOUT THE POET
Tatamkhulu Afrika was born in Egypt, the son of an Arabian father and a Turkish mother. He lived in South Africa from 1923, served in the Second World War and worked in the mines of Namibia. He converted to Islam in the 1960s and joined those resisting Apartheid. He was arrested in 1987 and banned for five years.

Sounds in 'Nothing's Changed'

This is a poem that makes use of all the devices we are looking at in this unit. We can find some examples of alliteration, assonance, sibilance and onomatopoeia just in the first stanza.

The first stanza

Alliteration

'cuffs, cans,
trodden on, crunch'

Here we have the hard 'c' sound repeated three times in 'cuffs', 'cans' and 'crunch'.

Once you have identified the technique you need to be able to comment on it as you did with the techniques from 'Blessing'.

Activity 2.9b   Discuss the effect of the use of the repeated hard 'c' sounds in 'cuffs, cans,/ trodden on, crunch'. Think about:

- the relationship between the sound of the 'c' and the meaning of the words they are in
- whether the sound is suited to what the poet is saying here.

Assonance and sibilance

'under my heels,
seeding grasses thrust
bearded seeds …'

Here we have repeated 's' sounds, many of which do not come at the beginnings of words. Five of the eight words here have at least one 's' in them so the whole feel of the lines is one of rustling.

Activity 2.9c   Why do you think the poet wants to create the rustling sound here? Does it fit in with what he is trying to say?

Onomatopoeia

'Small round hard stones click'

As with alliteration above, the poet uses hard sounds here – 'd', 't' and 'c' – to create the effect he wants. The whole of the first stanza is used to create the setting and atmosphere for the poem. Apart from the scene setting we do not know anything except that a person is walking in this setting.

Activity 2.9d   Using the notes you made about alliteration, sibilance, assonance and onomatopoeia, what kind of atmosphere and setting do you think the poet is trying to create? Do you think the first stanza is effective?

 BACKGROUND INFORMATION
Apartheid was a political system in South Africa run by white people and based on the segregation of the people of other races from the white people, who occupied a much more privileged position in every respect.

Why does the poet make so much use of techniques that highlight sounds?
In working on the last three activities you will have had to think about the meaning of the poem and what the poet's purposes might have been in writing it.

You will probably agree that the poem is about racial prejudice and the separation of white and black people which was a feature of South Africa under **apartheid**. The poem deals with the poet's feelings about observing the privileged white people enjoying an experience from which he and other ethnic groups were excluded. Tatamkhulu Afrika here uses all the devices at his command to make the reader feel what he felt in this situation.

The poem as a whole
The examples you have looked at so far in the first stanza are just a few of the sound effects the poet uses. Look now at the way he uses sound techniques in the poem as a whole.

Alliteration

You might write about alliteration in the poem as a whole like this:

As we have noted, the 'c' sounds in the example of alliteration from the first stanza are hard sounds and fit into a pattern of other hard sounds, such as the 'd' in 'hard', 'under' and 'seeding'. They pick up the hard 'c' of 'click' in the first line. You may notice that three of these words that begin with a hard 'c' come at the end of the line: 'click', 'cans' and 'crunch'. Both 'click' and 'crunch' are also onomatopoeic, evoking the sound of things trodden underfoot. That is entirely appropriate to a poem where the poet is reflecting on the way the black minority was trodden underfoot by the privileged white ruling class.

In the second stanza, the poet writes of 'the skin about my bones,/ and the soft labouring of my lungs'. Here he uses repeated hard 'b' sounds and repeated soft 'l' sounds. The 'b' sounds are called 'plosives'. These are sounds which are created by a release of air from the lips, a kind of small explosion. The effect here is to create a sense of the painful experience of exclusion which the speaker senses through the different parts of his body. The word 'labouring' suggests difficulty in breathing and 'bones' probably reminds us feeling something in our bones, a well-known saying. The repeated soft 'l' sounds add to the sense of pain and difficulty, because they linger on the tongue as we say them.

Assonance and sibilance

You could use the same quotation to illustrate both assonance and sibilance. Assonance is the repetition of vowel sounds and you need to notice whether the vowels are short or long. The repeated double 'e' in 'seeds' and 'seeding' gives a long, drawn out sound that may be seen to have a number of different effects:

- The repeated long sounds suggest length of time, perhaps the period during which certain ethnic groups have been subjugated by the white minority in South Africa.
- The sounds are also rather weary, suggesting the strain of the situation and the despair of anything ever changing.
- Two of the words are related to growth and natural things, 'seeds' and 'weeds'. As well as being examples of assonance, these words are also of course rhyming words. These two techniques that simultaneously connect the words may suggest that the downtrodden minority (the idea of being downtrodden is suggested by 'under my heels') are thrusting upwards and will eventually overtake the white minority.

Activity 2.9e   Find some other examples of assonance and sibilance in the rest of the poem. Comment on how they work and say how far you think they are appropriate to what the poet is saying.

Onomatopoeia

Again we find that words which are alliterative are also onomatopoeic, such as 'click' and 'crunch'. The sounds suggested by these words evoke an image of authority crushing people. The click of heels is particularly associated with the German Nazis.

Fitting these examples of techniques into a reading of the poem as a whole

It is always important to remember that we take things apart in order to understand them, but we also need to be able to put them together again afterwards. An example that is often given of this is of someone taking a clock to pieces, but not knowing how to put it back together afterwards.

The process of taking a piece of literature apart is called **analysis**. The process of seeing it as a whole is called **synthesis**. We have looked at some of the techniques that use sound to affect our understanding of the poem. Think about these techniques in conjunction with other aspects we have discussed in previous units, before getting an overall picture of the poem.

Activity 2.9f   Explore the way Tatamkhulu Afrika uses:

- imagery
- contrast
- structure
- punctuation
- repetition other than that involved in alliteration, assonance and sibilance.

Hints

- Look at the kind of simple visual imagery to be found in the poem. One example would be 'tall, purple-flowering,/amiable weeds'.
- The poem is based on the contrast between the lives of black and white people. What other contrasts does the poet use to highlight the central contrast of the poem?
- The use of contrast is in itself part of the poem's structure. Examine how other aspects, for instance the stanza form, also give structure to the poem.
- The way a writer uses punctuation affects the way you read the text. How has the writer used punctuation here and what effects does its use have?
- Repetition also helps to give structure as well as emphasis. Examine how it is used here.

Serious practice

UNIT ACTIVITY 2.9   Write about either 'Nothing's Changed' or 'Blessing', commenting on the way the poet uses two of the sound techniques we have discussed here and two of the other techniques listed in Activity 2.9f. Try to relate all the techniques to the purpose they have in the poem and how far they help the poet to achieve it.

WHAT EXAMINERS ARE LOOKING FOR
By this stage, you should be able to deal with a number of different techniques in a piece of writing. For a C grade, you need to make relevant comment on 'methods of presentation/ language and their effects'.

Unit 2.10
Rhythm and metre

The unit activity is to write about the way in which Imtiaz Dharker creates rhythm in 'This Room' and what the effect is (see page 135).

Making a start

In Unit 2.9, we discussed the sound of poetry and, of course, the sound we hear depends a lot on the rhythm and metre of the poem.

What is rhythm?

Unit 2.1 pointed out the importance of rhythm to poetry, but in fact rhythm is important to all living things. Rhythm is produced by a recurrent pattern. For example, your body has its own rhythm determined by your heartbeat. It gives a shape to your life in the same way that rhythm gives shape to a poem. The recurrent pattern in poetry is produced by recurring stressed and unstressed syllables.

Rhythm in pre-twentieth century poetry

Rhythmic patterns in older poetry were usually much more regular than they are in modern poetry. The two most likely patterns you may come across are:

*   repeated **iambs**, which is where an unstressed syllable is followed by a stressed syllable, for example, 'To-morrow, and to-morrow, and to-morrow'
*   repeated **trochees**, which is the other way around – a stressed syllable is followed by an unstressed syllable, for example, 'Tiger! Tiger! Burning bright/ In the forests of the night'.

Iambic pentameter

'To-morrow, and to-morrow, and to-morrow' is from Shakespeare's *Macbeth* and, if you are not familiar with it already, you may well study it during your GCSE course.

The first syllable is unstressed ('To'), the second stressed ('morr') and the pattern continues alternately to the end of the line. The line ends on an unstressed syllable because, although the line Shakespeare uses basically has ten syllables, he alters it a great deal to achieve the effects he wants.

The ten-syllable line Shakespeare uses is called an **iambic pentameter**.

Trochaic tetrameter

'Tiger! Tiger! Burning bright' is from a poem called 'The Tiger' by William Blake, an eighteenth-century poet and the first of a group that came to be called the Romantic Poets.

Blake's rhythmic pattern here is of a stressed syllable followed by an unstressed syllable. This is basically an eight-syllable line but, like Shakespeare, Blake alters it for his own purposes. He cuts out the last unstressed syllable, ending the line in a strong and emphatic way.

The eight-syllable line Blake uses is called a **trochaic tetrameter**.

Activity 2.10a   Look at these two quotations

a) 'Now they ride the wintry dawn' (from 'Under Ben Bulben'
   by the Irish poet W.B. Yeats)
b) 'If I should die, think only this of me' (from 'The Soldier'
   by Rupert Brooke).

Work out what sort of metrical pattern they have.

Hints

- How many syllables are there in the line?
- What is the pattern of stressed and unstressed syllables?
- If there are ten syllables grouped in pairs, the line is a pentameter.
- If there are eight syllables grouped in pairs, the line is a tetrameter.

The poetry from different cultures that you are studying has few examples of iambic or trochaic rhythm in the sense that earlier poets would have used them. However, it helps to understand the ways in which English was used in the twentieth century if you have some idea of the patterns of stresses used by the poets of earlier eras.

IAMBIC RHYTHM IN EVERYDAY SPEECH

The pattern of an unstressed syllable followed by a stressed one – the iambic pattern – is basic to English speech. Lots of the ordinary things you say everyday have this rhythm.

For instance, if you said 'He went outside to get his bike', you would be using iambic rhythm.

Rhythm in modern poetry

In the twentieth century poets started to be much more free and flexible in their use of rhythm. They stopped making sure that they had more or less the same number of syllables per line and more or less the same number of stressed and unstressed syllables.

RHYTHM ... OR NO RHYTHM?

Beware of thinking that the lack of a regular rhythm means that a poem has no rhythm at all. Candidates in examinations often write that a poem has no rhythm, when what they really mean is that it does not have a *regular* rhythmic pattern to which we give a particular name.

If a poem seems completely shapeless and without rhythmic power, then arguably it is not a poem at all. That is, however, a controversial issue that you could debate.

Culture and rhythm

The changing attitude towards rhythm and metre in the twentieth century is one effect of culture change on poetry. Since you are studying poems from different cultures, you will be aware that another aspect of cultural change is to do with ethnic groups writing in English in other countries or settling in the UK and producing poetry in English here. They are obviously influenced by the patterns of life of their original cultures so that eventually they become a part of the British culture.

The rhythm of rap: 'Limbo'

Rap music, which originated among black people in the USA, is an example of a different kind of rhythm that has come to have great effect on British society. You can see its influence in poetry, for instance, in Edward Kamau Brathwaite's 'Limbo' (page 88).

Edward Kamau Brathwaite was influenced by West Indian rhythmic patterns and, in this poem, by the rhythms of rap music, an art form that involves the quick rhythmic uttering of words over a background of music. West Indian steel bands or drums often give the backing to rap and their influence can also be felt in the poem.

Music or poetry?

You may wonder what music has to do with the study of poetry but it has been pointed out that 'Limbo' is very effective when sung or chanted and would also be effective with a musical backing. Poems have often been put to music over the centuries.

Activity 2.10b   In groups, discuss what evidence you can find in 'Limbo' that the poet is thinking about music as well as words.

Hints

Consider:

♦ the meaning of 'limbo'
♦ the references to musical instruments
♦ the importance of dancing.

So the focus of the poem is very much one that combines the speaking/singing voice of the speaker with a suggested musical backing.

Working out the rhythmic pattern

What you have to work out is the relationship between the rhythm of the poem, the sense of a musical backing and the culture the poem is based in. Look at the first line of 'Limbo':

'And limbo stick is the silence in front of me'

There are different ways in which the line could be said, but you will probably agree that there are:

* two stressed syllables in 'limbo'
* one on 'stick'
* one on the first syllable of 'silence'
* one on 'front'
* one on 'me'.

If you write the line out indicating where the stressed and unstressed syllables would go if you read it aloud like that, this is what it looks like:

And **lim-bo stick** is the **sil**-ence in **front** of **me**.

You will notice that the stresses are not regular as in iambic rhythm. There are three stressed syllables in a row on the words 'limbo stick', which help to give the strong, insistent rhythm we associate with West Indian culture. The vitality of it comes partly from those stresses, but also from repeated unstressed syllables, as in 'ence in'. The combination of frequent stresses and frequent unstressed syllables gives a feeling of vibrancy and motion.

Activity 2.10c   1   How does the poet use repetition to establish the rhythm we have just explored? Find:

- any lines which have identical or almost identical rhythmic patterns
- any lines where the words are identical
- any repeated rhythms in the poem, such as groups of words that are all stressed or stressed syllables with two unstressed syllables between them.

2   What do you think is the effect of the uses of repetition you have found?

How does the rhythm relate to what the poet is saying?

We have looked in some detail at how the rhythm of 'Limbo' works. A very important aspect you need to think about is how far the rhythm is appropriate to what the poet is saying. Poets choose different rhythms to say different things.

Activity 2.10d   In a group, work out what you think Edward Kamau Brathwaite is saying in 'Limbo'. What is his main point? Is he trying to get a message across to his readers?

What happens in the poem?

This is another question we have to ask, but it is not easy to answer because, by overlapping past and present situations, the poet makes his words somewhat ambiguous. You might say that what happens is that while dancing the speaker feels himself in touch with his ancestors and the feeling is so strong that he has a kind of vision and almost becomes one of his ancestors, experiencing what they experienced.

They were whipped and the poet connects the limbo stick and the whip to make a link between past and present. He imagines himself to be on the deck of a ship on the ocean in the dark. The drummer playing for the limbo dance seems to call him, to raise him out of the dark to the sunlight and to save him from his terrible fate.

He may mean that the music of the African people and their belief in their gods enabled his ancestors to cope with their terrible situation and now creates a link between him and them because the music is part of an ongoing tradition in their culture. However torturous the situation suggested by 'the burning ground', the music carries him to some kind of salvation.

Activity 2.10e   You may have a different view of what happens in the poem. Discuss the ideas above in a group. Do you agree with them or do you have some other ideas?

Serious practice

Free verse: 'This Room'

The kind of rhythm we have found in 'Limbo' is quite specialised. Most of the poets in this collection write in **free verse.**

Hints

Ask yourself:

♦ What is the setting for the poem?

- Is there just one setting or is there more than one?
- Is the speaker really on a 'long dark deck' with 'the water surrounding me'?
- If not, why does he mention that other setting and what setting is he actually in?

♦ What situation is the poet writing about?

- If there is more than one setting, is there more than one situation?
- If so, what situations are there?

♦ Who is the speaker of the poem?

- Is the speaker the poet?
- Or is the speaker putting himself into the role of someone else? If he is, he is taking on a **persona**.
- Is it possible that the speaker can be both the poet and someone else simultaneously?

FREE VERSE

This is verse which is written using the rhythms of the speaking voice rather than the set rhythm of iambic or trochaic metre. As pointed out before that does not mean it is the same as prose, because poets use many other devices to give a sense of rhythm to poetry, including

enjambement

The omission of punctuation to allow one line to flow freely into the next.

end-stopped line

The use of punctuation to create a pause at the end of the line.

caesura

A pause within a line, usually indicated by punctuation.

line length

This may vary greatly within a poem but you should assume that the poet had a purpose in choosing to make each line as long or as short as it is.

Many of the poems in this collection do not have any punctuation at all, so you do not need to think about how they have used punctuation but about *why they have chosen not to use it and what the effect of their choice is.*

This Room

This room is breaking out
of itself, cracking through
its own walls
in search of space, light,
empty air.   5

The bed is lifting out of
its nightmares.
From dark corners, chairs
are rising up to crash through clouds.

This is the time and place   10
to be alive:
when the daily furniture of our lives
stirs, when the improbable arrives.
Pots and pans bang together
in celebration, clang   15
past the crowd of garlic, onions, spices,
fly by the ceiling fan.
No one is looking for the door.

In all this excitement
I'm wondering where   20
I've left my feet and why

my hands are outside, clapping.

Imtiaz Dharker
(India)

'This Room' on page 136 is an example of a poem in free verse. Imtiaz Dharker uses the rhythms of ordinary speech, but it is worthwhile looking at the way she uses:

- line length
- enjambement
- end-stopped lines
- caesura.

Line length

First stanza

If you read the first stanza just as a prose sentence, it makes grammatical sense, but if you look at the way the poet has divided up the lines you may see more in it.

To begin with, the poem is quite strange and rather surreal because it suggests that the room and the furniture go in search of some kind of fulfilment. It makes quite good sense if you think of it as perhaps saying that as people we tend to live in quite constraining circumstances (for example, cooped up in a room metaphorically-speaking) and that when life offers us a chance to change our lives in some radical way we should take it.

The fact that the poem is so metaphorical and surreal seems perhaps to make it more suited to poetic form than prose anyway.

Second stanza

If you look at the second stanza, you might decide that the poet divides the lines up as she does to give a sense of movement and rising. The first line stresses 'lifting' in contrast to the 'nightmares' of the second line. The third line picks up on the feel of nightmares with 'dark corners' only to move into the last line's strong upward escaping movement, 'rising up to crash through clouds'. The way the two lines expressing free movement enclose the two related to dark and nightmares suggests the triumph of liberation over imprisonment.

Activity 2.10f   Take the other three devices, enjambement, end-stopped lines and caesura.

1   Discuss them in relation to 'This Room'.
2   Write about them in a similar way to the discussion of line length above.

Hints   As a guide, here are examples of each technique:

- Enjambement:
  'This room is breaking out
  Of itself,'

- End-stopped line:
  The last lines of stanza one and two are end-stopped.

- Caesura:
  'past the crowd of garlic, onions, spices,'

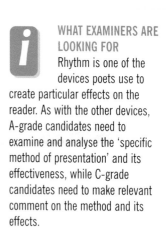 **WHAT EXAMINERS ARE LOOKING FOR**
Rhythm is one of the devices poets use to create particular effects on the reader. As with the other devices, A-grade candidates need to examine and analyse the 'specific method of presentation' and its effectiveness, while C-grade candidates need to make relevant comment on the method and its effects.

UNIT ACTIVITY 2.10   Write about the rhythm of 'This Room', looking at the use of free verse and devices such as those you looked at in Activity 2.10f. Say whether you think the poet puts across her message effectively.

Unit 2.11

Exam focus: 1

The unit activity is to write a comparison of the ways two poets use imagery (see page 143).

Making a start

We have looked at a wide range of poems to explore both what they are about and also the ways in which the poets put across their ideas and feelings. Finally, you need to work at drawing together the right material to answer an examination question before writing the answer itself.

Comparing poems

In Units 2.7 and 2.8, we looked at Sujata Bhatt's lines from 'Search For My Tongue' (page 116) and Tom Leonard's lines from 'Unrelated Incidents' (page 117). We discovered in Unit 2.7 that these two poems have the following things in common:

- The central issue for both of them is identity.
- They both see identity as closely connected with language.
- They both use their own language or dialect in the poem.

One of the skills you need when planning to write an effective essay is to collect appropriate evidence from the poems you are comparing.

MAKING A COMPARISON

GCSE questions on poetry require you to *compare* two poems. Remember that to compare means to find:

- the similarities between the two
- the ways in which they are different.

In other words you have to do what is often called *comparing and contrasting*.

If the poems have nothing in common, there is little point in contrasting them. What examiners want you to do is to look at the very different ways in which poets approach similar subjects and concerns.

You have worked on comparison throughout your work in the previous units, because you have looked at:

- different kinds of language
- different kinds of imagery
- different stanza forms
- different layouts on the page
- rhyme or no rhyme
- different rhythms
- different viewpoints and tones
- different concerns.

Now you need to draw that work together in a more sustained way.

Activity 2.11a   Which textual evidence might you use to illustrate the three points made above?
Copy and complete the table to compile your evidence.

Concern	Evidence	
	'Search For My Tongue'	'Unrelated Incidents'
Central issue of identity	1 'I have lost my tongue' 2 3	1 'yi/ widny wahnt/ mi ti talk/ aboot thi/ trooth wia/ voice lik/ wanna yoo/ scruff' 2 3
Connection between language and identity	1 'the mother tongue' 2 3	1 'this/ is me tokn yir/ right way a/ spellin' Any example will do since the whole poem is in Glaswegian dialect
Use of own language or dialect in the poem	1 the use of Gujerati 2 3	

You have now compiled some textual evidence. What you need to do next is to put into your own words what you think the poems have in common, using quotation to back up your point.

THE GOLDEN RULES OF QUOTING

- Make sure your quotation is accurate.
- Use quotation as briefly as possible to get your point across.
- It is much better to weave the quotation into the sentence you are writing than to set it out separately.

These rules are particularly important because you can take your Anthology into the examination with you, so you are not proving anything by long quotations and there is no excuse for inaccuracy.

The close connection between language and identity

When you compare poems, it is best not to write more than a few sentences about one before you bring the other in to show the similarities or differences. You can start by writing two or three sentences that make one point and that include some evidence from both poems, for example:

'Search For My Tongue' and 'Unrelated Incidents' are both centrally concerned with the connection between language and identity. Sujata Bhatt shows this by equating the tongue in her mouth with language, her original language being her 'mother tongue', while English is 'a foreign tongue'. Tom Leonard, on the other hand, makes his point through the use of Glaswegian dialect which, while it makes him the individual he is, also distances him from the news reader, who has a BBC accent and whom he sees as looking down on him as 'wonna yoo scruff'.

The pattern established here is a good one to follow:

- The first sentence establishes what the two poems have in common.
- The second sentence illustrates the common element from the first poem.
- The third sentence shows how differently the other poem presents the same concern.

Activity 2.11b

1. In a group, see how many different points you can find to make about the different kinds of language used in the two poems. Copy and complete the table.

Different kinds of language in:	
'Search For My Tongue	**'Unrelated Incidents'**
1 formal English	1 very informal English
2 complete sentences	2
3	3
4 phonetic spelling – transliteration	4
5	5 very little metaphorical language

2. Using the points you have collected, write a paragraph on one of them showing the common or contrasting element and illustrating your point from both poems. Write in clear, accurate English and include some quotation.

Hint

Use a table like the one above to compare any area of difference in the pairs of poems you are working on. See the list of areas of difference on page 138.

The effect of language used

The paragraph you have written should make a clear comparison but you have not as yet commented on the effect of the different kinds of language the poets use. To get the highest grade, you need to comment on the effect of language.

Consider, for example, the different effects achieved by using formal English rather than informal English. The following table suggests some of the effects of formal English in 'Search For My Tongue'. The first point made is that Sujata Bhatt's formal English gives the impression of an educated person. Think about the rather different effect of Tom Leonard's Scottish dialect. You might say that the Scottish dialect suggests that the speaker is not well-educated.

The effect of formal English in 'Search For My Tongue'	The effect of informal English in 'Unrelated Incidents'
1 Gives the reader the impression that the poet's English is of a high standard.	1
2 Enables the poet to express complex thoughts in complex images, which reinforces our admiration for her skills.	2
3 Helps to present a contrast with the Gujerati, which is sandwiched between two sections in formal English.	3
4 Suggests that, although the poet is suffering because of her divided identity, she is not a natural rebel.	4

You might have found different reasons why the poets use formal or informal English and they may have had quite different effects on you as a reader. As long as you can back up your view with evidence from the text, you will get credit for your viewpoint. In the case of Tom Leonard's use of Glaswegian dialect, your response will depend on individual factors, such as your own position in the class system, your political views, and so on.

Activity 2.11c

1 Complete the table to show the effects of Tom Leonard's dialect, non-standard English. Think about:

- how the use of dialect reflects the speaker's values
- what tone of voice comes across
- whether the dialect gives the impression of an individual voice.

2 Write a paragraph that includes some comparison of the ways the poets use language and also gives some comment on the effect of the language used.

Comparing imagery

One of the most difficult things to do is to write about the images poets use and their effects. For practice in this, reread 'Island Man' by Grace Nichols and 'Blessing' by Imtiaz Dharker opposite.

Island Man

Morning
and island man wakes up
to the sound of blue surf
in his head
the steady breaking and wombing   5

wild seabirds
and fishermen pushing out to sea
the sun surfacing defiantly
from the east
of his small emerald island   10
he always comes back   groggily groggily

Comes back to sands
of a grey metallic soar
                    to surge of wheels
to dull North Circular roar   15

muffling muffling
his crumpled pillow waves
island man heaves himself

Another London day

Grace Nichols
(Guyana)

Blessing

The skin cracks like a pod
There never is enough water.

Imagine the drip of it,
the small splash, echo
in a tin mug   5
the voice of a kindly god.

Sometimes, the sudden rush
of fortune. The municipal pipe bursts,
silver crashes to the ground
and the flow has found   10
a roar of tongues. From the huts,
a congregation: every man and woman
child for streets around
butts in, with pots,
brass, copper, aluminium,   15
plastic buckets,
frantic hands,

and naked children
screaming in the liquid sun,
their highlights polished to perfection,   20
flashing light,
as the blessing sings
over their small bones.

Imtiaz Dharker
(India)

Metaphor and simile

The most difficult kind of images to unpack are metaphors and similes, which both make comparisons, as you saw in Unit 2.8.

Activity 2.11d

1 In a group, see how many comparisons you can find in the two poems. Copy and complete the table.

Metaphors and similes in 'Island Man'	What is being compared with what?
1 '… island man wakes up to the sound of blue surf in his head'	1 The actual sound of the surf on the island beaches of the man's home is compared with the imagined sound in his head. The words 'sound of blue surf' are odd because surf is white and because the word order suggests that he can hear the colour blue.
2 'the steady breaking and wombing'	
3 'his crumpled pillow waves'	

2 Compile a similar table for 'Blessing'.
3 Are the metaphors are well chosen? Are they apt?

The metaphor of water

In 'Blessing', you probably found that the poet uses a lot of metaphors for water. She compares water with 'the voice of a kindly god', with 'the sudden rush of fortune',with 'silver' crashing and perhaps most importantly with 'a blessing'.

Consider the metaphor of water as a blessing:

- What do you think 'blessing' normally means?
- Which aspect of life do you connect the word 'blessing' with?
- What is there about water that makes it a 'blessing'?
- Why do you think the poet gives the poem the title 'Blessing'? Would it have made any difference if she had called it 'Water'?
- Overall, do you think the idea of water as a 'blessing' here is apt?

The meaning of 'blessing'

If you asked a number of people what 'blessing' means, you would probably get a variety of answers. For instance, some might just say it means something good and helpful, while others might see it in a religious sense, a gift from God.

Activity 2.11e

1 Each member of your group could ask half a dozen people, preferably covering a range of ages and occupations, how they would define the word 'blessing'.

2 Put your results together and consider how far the meanings different people have suggested relate to what you think the meaning is in the poem.

Which aspect of life do you connect the word 'blessing' with?
A blessing is the name given to a prayer, often spoken at the conclusion
of a religious service. The prayer is one that asks for God's love and protection.
People who are concerned with religion are therefore likely to connect the
word 'blessing' with religious observance.

Activity 2.11f   What is it about water that makes it a 'blessing'? Thinking of the word here in
the more practical way as something helpful and good, make a list of the ways
in which the poem shows water to be a 'blessing'.

The title

Why might the poet have chosen this title? And is it a good one? It might be
said that the title helps the reader to make a connection between the flow of
water and something that comes from God. Even though the flow of water is
not rain, which might most obviously be seen as being sent by God, but rather
a burst 'municipal pipe', the poet suggests that man is just a channel through
which the water given by God flows. If the poet had simply called the poem
'Water', the religious element would have been lost, suggesting perhaps that
what happens to us is entirely to do with our own efforts and actions.

Your response may of course be quite different from the one given here.
It might well depend on whether you have any religious beliefs. Even if you
have not, however, you may be able to see what the poem means in the context
of Imtiaz Dharker's own beliefs.

Comparing imagery

This is an example of a paragraph comparing the imagery of 'Island Man' and
'Blessing':

> *Both poets are concerned with the sound of water. This is closely
> connected with the use of metaphor. Grace Nichols writes of 'the
> sound of blue surf', while Imtiaz Dharker says 'silver crashes to the
> ground'. Both make use of colour here, 'silver' perhaps
> metaphorically suggesting the value of the water as well as its
> appearance. The onomatopoeic word 'crashes' gives a similar effect
> to Grace Nichols' use of the words 'surf'. The odd word order, 'the
> sound of blue surf' makes it seem as if the blueness of the sea can
> be heard. This mixing of two different senses in an image is called
> SYNAESTHESIA and makes the image, although it is simple, seem vivid
> and intense. The senses coming together highlights the island
> man's nostalgia for his homeland.*

Serious practice

UNIT ACTIVITY 2.11   Compare the different ways the two poets use imagery in 'Island Man'
and 'Blessing'. Both use imagery of water in their own individual ways.

i   **WHAT EXAMINERS ARE
LOOKING FOR**
By this stage, you
should be able to write
about all the devices poets use and
the ability to compare the ways two
poets use one of these devices is
introduced here. You are now
looking to fulfil the assessment
objective which requires you to
'understand and evaluate how
writers use linguistic, structural
and presentational devices to
achieve their effects'. If you can
'evaluate', that is discuss at a high
level, you will be able to obtain an
A grade. For a C grade, you need to
be able to make 'relevant
comparison of methods of
presentation/ language and their
effects'.

Unit 2.12

Exam focus: 2

The unit activity is to write an answer to an examination-style question (see page 150).

Compare the ways in which the poets present people in 'Two Scavengers in a Truck' and **one** other poem of your choice from the Poems from Different Cultures and Traditions.

Write about:

- what the different people are like
- what the poets think about them
- how the language brings out what the people are like
- how the language shows what the poets think about the people
- which poem you prefer and why.

Making a start

In this unit, we are going to look at the examination-type question on the left. This is an exemplar question for Foundation Tier. The equivalent question for Higher Tier is the same, but no bullet points are given.

Finding a method

Identifying the key words

It is much easier to tackle an examination question if you have a method that you always follow. You will, of course, have more time to do everything thoroughly when you are answering questions for homework rather than in the exam. The first two things you need to do are:

- read the question carefully a couple of times
- underline the key words.

The **key words** are the most important words – those which tell you exactly what it is that you are being asked to do. In the question given above, the key words are:

- 'compare'
- 'ways'
- 'poets'
- 'present people'
- 'Two Scavengers in a Truck'
- '**one** other poem'.

Whatever the question is, there will be key words of a similar nature to those given here.

The key words are closely linked to the Assessment Objectives, for example:

- One of your Assessment Objectives is to:

Understand and evaluate how writers use linguistic, structural and presentational devices to achieve their effects, and comment on the ways language changes and varies.

Three of the important words in this assessment objective are 'how writers use'. That means that you have to identify the techniques used by writers and comment on their purposes. These are the things you have been practising throughout the units in this book. In the exam, you have to put them into effect. The words equivalent to 'how writers use' in the question are 'ways in which poets present'. There will always be some words in the question you are given such as 'use', 'present' and 'ways' which guide you to talk about the poet's techniques and how they work.

- The key word 'compare' is linked to another of the Assessment Objectives:

Select material appropriate to purpose, collate material from different sources, and make cross references.

By asking you to compare two poems the examiner is making sure that you fulfil this objective by taking relevant material from both poems and showing how they relate to one another, for instance by dealing with the same concerns but presenting them in different ways.

The other key words, 'Two Scavengers in a Truck' and '**one** other poem' are the words which tell you which poem or poems to deal with. Every question will have a named poem in it, which you will have been taught. The 'other poem' can be taken from either of the two clusters of poems dealing with different cultures in the Anthology.

If your answer deals with all these key words it stands a good chance of gaining a high mark.

Choosing your poem

In this particular question, the next step in your method should be to pick a suitable poem to compare with the one given.

You could pick any of the poems you have studied, because all these poems are to some extent about people. However, some of them would give you more scope than others for answering this particular question. For instance, 'Presents from my Aunts in Pakistan' gives quite a detailed portrayal of the girl who receives the presents, whereas 'This Room' is more concerned with a situation and, although it deals with people's reactions it is very generalised. You may pick your second poem partly on the basis of what you like and what you know best, but make sure it is a suitable choice for the particular question. For the purposes of this unit, we shall compare the given poem with 'Not My Business' by Niyi Osundare (page 103).

Foundation Tier

What the different people are like and what the poets think about them

COMPARING POEMS

One useful way of comparing is to make two columns and then note points relating to relevant aspects of each poem so that you can glance across and easily see where the similarities and differences are.

Activity 2.12a

1. Make a list of points relating to what the people are like in 'Two Scavengers in a Truck' (page 146) and 'Not My Business' (page 103). Copy and complete the table, adding any relevant points you can find.

'Two Scavengers in a Truck'	'Not My Business'
1 Two different pairs of people: garbagemen on a truck and an 'elegant' couple in a Mercedes.	1 Two different sets of people: working people and police or security people who abuse them
2 Americans	2
3	3 No details of what any of the people look like.
4 All young people except for one garbageman.	4

Two Scavengers in a Truck,
Two Beautiful People in a Mercedes

At the stoplight waiting for the light
    nine a.m. downtown San Francisco
a bright yellow garbage truck
   with two garbagemen in red plastic blazers
standing on the back stoop   5
    one on each side hanging on
and looking down into
    an elegant open Mercedes
  with an elegant couple in it

The man   10
  in a hip three-piece linen suit
   with shoulder-length blond hair & sunglasses
The young blond woman so casually coifed
    with a short skirt and colored stockings
on the way to his architect's office   15

And the two scavengers up since four a.m.
     grungy from their route
  on the way home
The older of the two with grey iron hair
     and hunched back   20
  looking down like some
    gargoyle Quasimodo
And the younger of the two
    also with sunglasses & long hair
about th same age as the Mercedes driver 25

And both scavengers gazing down
     as from a great distance
  at the cool couple
as if they were watching some odorless TV ad
  in which everything is always possible 30

And the very red light for an instant
   holding all four close together
  as if anything at all were possible
     between them
across that small gulf   35
   in the high seas
    of this democracy

Lawrence Ferlinghetti
(USA)

Activity 2.12a
continued

2 List your responses for 'what the poets think of the people' in two columns:

'Two Scavengers in a Truck'	'Not My Business'
1 The poet thinks these two sets of people could never really get on together or understand one another.	1 The poet thinks some people treat those under them without humanity and compassion.
2	2
3	3
4	4

How the language brings out what the people are like

Look for the words that describe people and things. In the first stanza of 'Two Scavengers', the following adjectives are used: 'downtown', 'bright', 'yellow', 'red', 'plastic', 'back', 'elegant' (twice) and 'open'. You need to think about how helpful the adjectives are in enabling the reader to visualise the scene. The colours, for instance, are vivid and give us a good idea of how bright the binmen and their truck would look. If you look at some of the other adjectives in the poem, such as 'grungy' and 'grey iron' you can see that there is a clear contrast between the bright primary colours of the inanimate aspects of the scene and the grey, dull presentation of the men themselves.

The adjectives discussed here are all from one poem, but they give you the opportunity to compare because the particular poem is based on a contrast. Now think about the adjectives in 'Not My Business'.

Activity 2.12b

1 Pick out the adjectives used by Niyi Osundare.
2 Are they similar to or different from the adjectives used by Ferlinghetti?
3 Write about the differences, trying to work out why the two poets use adjectives in different ways.

> **Hint**
>
> For instance, you might comment on the way Ferlinghetti uses the word 'elegant' twice, while Osundare repeats 'savouring' three times.

How the language shows the poets' viewpoints

If you look closely at the language it also tells you what the poet's viewpoint is. To start with, the language of 'Two Scavengers' conveys a contrast between the binmen and the couple in the car. The couple are 'elegant' while the binmen are 'scrungy' for instance. However, do not make the mistake of assuming that the poet thinks the couple are superior to the binmen. The last part of the poem shows, not that the poet has anything against the elegant couple, but that he realises that in a so-called democratic society there are divisions between people that are impossible to get rid of. The image of the four together at the end of the poem just before the traffic lights change and the words 'as if' show that the poet does not think different kinds of people in society will ever really come together.

Activity 2.12c

1 Decide what the poet's viewpoint is in 'Not My Business'.
2 Is it the same all the way through the poem?
3 In what ways is it similar to or different from Ferlinghetti's viewpoint?

Which poem you prefer and why

Finally, you need to decide which poem you prefer and be able to say why. You might be more interested in one set of people than another, or you might prefer the language or layout of one poem over the other.

Higher Tier

If you are doing a Higher Tier exam you do not get the help of bullet points, so you need to think about which aspects the key words are asking you to concentrate on. If you are comparing, follow the same method of columns. You need to think in terms of:

• subject-matter or concerns
• the poet's methods, such as use of language, imagery, tone, and so on.

The subject-matter we are concerned with here is people, so you need to be aware of what kind of people the poet presents to us and what he is saying about them, i.e. what his view of them is. The poets will show that through the techniques they use. You need to identify those techniques and say what effect they have.

AN EXAMPLE OF COMPARISON

The title indicates that the poet's concern is the contrast between two pairs of people. By referring to the bin men as 'scavengers', he suggests that they get their living by trawling through rubbish rather than that they collect rubbish as a job. This makes a more effective contrast with the 'beautiful' young people in the car, which is reinforced by the description of the bin men as 'grungy'. The suggestion of being dirty and unkempt is a world away from the young woman's grooming; the alliterative 'casually coifed' emphasises the effortlessness of her appearance. Amongst the welter of contrasts, the poet cleverly describes both young men as having 'sunglasses and long hair', the similarity in appearance just highlighting the gulf between their social positions.

Activity 2.12d

1 Follow the same method outlined for Foundation Tier to work out what the people in the poems are like and what the poet thinks about them (Activity 2.12a).

2 Choose one point from the table, such as the first point about the people in 'Two Scavengers'. Look at the language that reveals them to us. Identify examples. Copy and complete the table adding other relevant points.

Garbagemen	Couple in Mercedes'
1 'scavengers'	1 'beautiful'
2 wear 'red plastic blazers'	2 young man wears 'a hip three-piece linen suit',young woman 'a short skirt and colored stockings'
3 'grungy'	3
4 one has 'grey iron hair'	4
5 sunglasses and long hair	5

3 Once you have identified the appropriate examples, think about whether the language is effective, and why.

Activity 2.12e Pick a different example from your list and write a paragraph using the example on the left as a model.

The poet's view

In establishing the contrast above we mentioned 'the gulf between their social positions'. It is important that you notice not only the contrast itself but the reason why it is there. You cannot decide whether the language is effective unless you have decided what you think the point of the poem is. The point might be to:

• show how immeasurably superior the couple in the Mercedes are to the bin men

- to show the limitations of a democratic society
- to show how difficult it is to bridge the gap between people in different social classes.

It would be possible to agree to some extent with any of these points.

Superiority

Whilst it seems unlikely that the poet is saying that the young couple are in any way superior as human beings to the bin men, he does seem to be saying that they are infinitely above them in social position, wealth and a sense of their own superiority. They seem to be presented as almost unreal, like people in TV advertisements whose lives are impossibly clean, pure and enviable, 'as if they were watching some odourless TV ad/ in which everything is always possible'. The lack of reality is highlighted by 'odorless' which suggests that they do not share the common humanity of the rest of us. Also, of course, it is a sharp contrast to the bin men, who must certainly be smelly after dealing with other people's rubbish.

The limitations of a democratic society

The poet certainly seems to suggest that democracy has its limitations in the conclusion of the poem. The two pairs are held in proximity 'for an instant' at the red light; the key words seem to be 'as if anything at all were possible'. The conditional 'as if' shows the poet's belief that the genuine coming together of these four people is not in fact possible. This, along with the metaphor of the 'small gulf/ in the high seas/ of this democracy' shows that he feels a genuine democracy is unattainable.

Activity 2.12f In a group, consider whether you agree that Ferlinghetti is showing the difficulty of bridging the gap between social classes.

> ### Hints
>
> You might consider:
>
> - the use of the simile 'like some/ gargoyle Quasimodo' with 'hunched back'
> - any other words or images that help to show the gulf between the two pairs.

The poet's tone

In finally deciding the poet's view you will find you need to assess the poet's tone. How does he speak of the young couple and of the two 'scavengers'? Is he scornful, approving, neutral, sympathetic? Reading tone is difficult and critics do not always agree on it. The first stanza may be seen as relatively neutral in simply describing the people concerned in such a way as to emphasise the contrast.

The second stanza, however, draws our attention through the patterning of the lines to the fact that the bin men have been up working since four a.m., while the young couple have presumably got up at a reasonable hour, showered, dressed and are on their way to an office. This is likely to make the reader feel sympathy for the bin men. Similarly the 'Quasimodo' image invites sympathy for the underdog and the superficial likeness of the two young men is likely to make us feel painfully aware of how little the young bin man has in his life. The last stanza has a rather wistful tone as the poet contemplates the different fates of individuals tossed on 'the high seas' of life.

Contrast with 'Not My Business'

We have looked at the comparisons within one of the two poems. Now we need to compare that poem with 'Not My Business'.

Activity 2.12g We have just been looking at tone and the poet's viewpoint in relation to 'Two Scavengers.' How are the tone and viewpoint different in 'Not My Business'?

Hints

You might consider whether:

- the first or third person is used
- you think the poems are based on the poets' personal experience
- the poets are revealing their personal feelings
- they are sympathetic or detached in what they write about
- you can find any suitable words to describe their tones of voice, such as 'sad', 'regretful', 'complacent' or 'remorseful'. Which words or phrases made you pick the words you did?

Descriptive detail

The people in 'Not My Business' are not described with any visual detail, unlike those in 'Two Scavengers'. Whereas Ferlinghetti concentrates on the public face of his characters, Osundare reveals the deeper feelings of his speaker. The other people in the poem are there to illustrate the speaker's responses. Rather than describe the speaker's appearance, the poet uses the repeated motif of the yam to highlight his ignorant selfishness.

The simile in the first stanza 'Beat him soft like clay', makes us aware of the yielding flesh of the man being beaten up, while the reference to 'clay' gives the idea that he is being moulded to the pattern dictated by society. The feelings of the speaker are most intense in the final stanza, with 'froze', hungry' and 'bewildered'.

You could continue here to say what the effect of these words is.

Differences in structure and layout

Activity 2.12h

1 The two poems look very different on the page. How does that affect your responses?
2 The layout of 'Two Scavengers' is unusual. Consider why the poet has such an irregular pattern both of line length and of positioning of lines.
3 It is also interesting that he uses no punctuation in his sentences yet starts each line with a capital letter. Why do you think this might be?

Serious practice

UNIT ACTIVITY 2.12   Write your own complete answer to the exam question on page 144.

Make your own choice of poem. Remember that if you are doing Higher Tier you will not have the bullet points.

WHAT EXAMINERS ARE LOOKING FOR
By now you can bring together all your skills and practise answering complete examination questions. You need to refer closely to the poems to give evidence. For a C grade, you need 'effective supporting use of textual detail, while for an A grade you need 'references integrated with argument'.

Glossary

alliteration

The repetition of a consonant in a line or lines of poetry, usually at the beginnings of words

assonance

The repetition of a vowel sound in a line or lines of poetry

bias

An inclination to favour one side or another in an argument; a viewpoint that is weighted towards a particular view or person

caesura

A pause within a line of poetry, usually indicated by punctuation

cartoon

A drawing done in a deliberately exaggerated way in order to make people laugh; often a form of satire

colloquialism

Non-standard use of English, such as 'He ain't coming'; often used more or less interchangeably with the word 'slang'

dialect

Usually refers to regional speech, but is also used to refer to the kinds of language that make up a 'social dialect' or an 'occupational dialect', an individual use of language for a particular group

end-stopped lines

The use of punctuation to create a pause at the end of a line of poetry

enjambement

The omission of punctuation to let one line flow freely into the next

first person

A text written in the first person uses 'I' or 'we' to express the viewpoint of the speaker directly. See also second person, third person

font

The kind of type used, which may vary in size or appearance

free verse

Verse which is written using the rhythms of the speaking voice rather than the set rhythm of iambic or trochaic metre

genre

A type of writing; newspaper writing is a genre just as poetry and drama are genres

image

Comparisons using similes and metaphors are images, but poets can also use purely descriptive imagery, which does not make comparisons

journalese

The kind of language used by newspapers in general

Latinate

Derived from the Latin language, for instance the word 'culture' derives from the Latin word cultura which means growing or cultivation

lexis

Words

masthead

The area across the top of the front page of a newspaper which displays the paper's name

metaphor

A comparison that does not use the word 'like' or 'as'

metonymy

A figure of speech in which a word is used as a substitute for something that is closely associated with it, for example, speaking of 'the Crown' to mean the Royal Family and the monarchy as a whole

non-fiction

Prose writing that is informative or factual rather than fictional

onomatopoeia
The use of a word which has a sound that echoes its meaning, such as 'splash', 'crash', 'drip'

patois
(pronounced *pat-wah*) A dialect common to the people of a region or country. For example, the English used by Jamaicans is a patois. It is Standard Jamaican English or Jamaican Creole

personification
Describing an inanimate object as if it were a person, as in 'The sun beamed down'

phonetic English
English written in a way that suggests the sounds of the words

prejudice
A preconceived opinion that is not based on rational consideration of the issues

register
The degree of formality of language used

rhetorical devices
Techniques used by writers to make their work effective, such as repetition, direct address to a listener or imagery

satire
Showing people's stupidities in a way that ridicules them, usually for humorous effect

second person
A text written in the second person uses the pronoun 'you' to addresses the reader directly

semantic field
Words used by a writer within a piece of text that relate to a common area of experience, such as war, cookery or precious gems

sibilance
Repeated 's' sounds in poetry

simile
A comparison between two things using the words 'like' or 'as'

slang
Very informal language, more often used in conversation than writing, such as 'bump off' instead of 'murder' or 'puke' instead of 'vomit'

standard English
The language as used by educated people with certain accepted conventions and rules

stanza
A unit of division in a poem, often called *verses*. Stanzas are usually of equal length; if of unequal length they are *verse paragraphs*

syllable
A unit of sound. If there is only one unit of sound, the word is *monosyllabic*; if there are two or more syllables, the word is *polysyllabic*

symbol
A word that stands for much more than just the object itself, for example, 'the cross' or 'a rose'

synaesthesia
The mixing of two different senses in an image

tabloidese
The language of tabloid newspapers

third person
A text written in the third person uses the pronouns 'he', 'she' or 'they'